STUDIES IN ENGLISH LITERATURE

Volume LXI

THE MORAL PARADOX
OF
PARADISE LOST

by

JOHN E. SEAMAN
University of Pacific

1971
MOUTON
THE HAGUE · PARIS

© Copyright 1971 in The Netherlands.
Mouton & Co. N.V., Publishers, The Hague.

LIBRARY OF CONGRESS CATALOG CARD NUMBER: 74-135665

Printed in The Netherlands by Mouton & Co., Printers, The Hague.

ACKNOWLEDGMENTS

A portion of Chapter I appeared in *English Studies* (April, 1968), and is reprinted here by permission. A portion of Chapter II appeared in *The Modern Language Review* 62 (1967), 212-13, and is reprinted here by permission of the Modern Humanities Research Association and of the Editors.

I wish to express my thanks to Professor Lawrence V. Ryan of Stanford University for his criticism and patience with the dissertation which was the original form of this book; to Professor Merritt Y. Hughes and Professor Standish Henning of the University of Wisconsin for valuable criticism of an earlier draft; to Professor George F. Sensabaugh of Stanford University, I owe a special debt of friendship and counsel for his careful supervision of the initial work and generosity in providing further criticism and encouragement which had much to do with the completion of the book; no less by his own example.

I wish to thank the Faculty Improvement Committee of Colorado State University for a generous grant which has defrayed part of the costs of publication.

Fort Collins, Colorado   J. E. S.
May 1968

CONTENTS

CONTENTS

INTRODUCTION

The modern reader of *Paradise Lost* can be forgiven for considering the poem a test of the patience and fortitude it celebrates.
As a classic, it is old, its structure and style unfamiliar, and it is
usually accompanied by footnotes alluding to a literature even
dustier. As an epic, it is formidably long, and this one – singing
of spiritual powers and the lost mythical paradise – seems remote
and difficult to a young audience often preoccupied with paradises more accessible. It is possible that *Paradise Lost* may some
day take its place beside the *Faerie Queene*, which even Renaissance scholars increasingly read in the spirit of an antiquarian.
When a valuable part of the past becomes alien or unintelligible,
the present, unfortunately, is often the loser.

In view of the energy, interest and sense of relevance among
Milton's interpreters today, however, the prospects hardly look
this dim. The spirit of Milton lives on at least in the contentious-
ness and independent spirit that have characterized the debate.
Whether or not this 'fit audience' are themselves read by other
than each other is another matter, but if the present loses touch
with this particular past, it will not be due to flagging interest
among Milton's interpreters. It is nevertheless an uncertain task
and an uphill struggle merely to strike a detente with history, in
whose impersonal grip the best often do not prevail and the good
die young. Ulysses is a good historian in pointing out the 'touch
of nature' that makes the 'whole world kin':

> That all with one consent praise new born gawds,
> Though they are made and molded of things past,
> And give to dust that is a little gilt

More laud than gilt o'erdusted.

(*Troilus and Cressida* III, iii)

It is possible to modernize Milton by dressing him in new styles, hopeful that he will no longer make a spectacle of himself on Times Square, but attempting to bring him forth thus newly born may be more provincial than the narrow historicism it tries to overcome; it is possible that the modern reader enlarges his experience more by the difficult process of adjusting his view to Milton's than by having Milton retailored. It is useful to approach the question of what *Paradise Lost* has to offer us on Milton's terms first.

It is therefore quite important that the light cast on Milton emulate the light from above, at least to the extent of distinguishing important features from peripheral and incidental ones. If Milton suffers by comparison to newborn gawds, and their composition of things past often goes unnoticed, it is perhaps because the challenge to separate the dust from the gold in Milton has not been fully met. Too often, neither past nor present appear in their true light, but rather in a negative conflict of ancient against modern, between ideas supposedly dead and pulses allegedly beating. If we should total up the many faces of Milton that appear in modern studies, we would have a curious gallery of disparate and inconsistent features: a stringent Puritanism, misogyny, heroic arrogance, a model of patient suffering, an underlying diabolism, not to mention others less respectable.

My interest is not in adding another portrait, but rather in reexamining the suffering servant model – so often attributed to Milton – and the heroic model – considered contradictory – offered him by the epic tradition. These models should be seen in the light of certain paradoxes which appear in Milton's perspective, and which have a more than incidental bearing on attempts to understand his concept of heroic virtue. The Renaissance was fond of paradox – as an intellectual exercise and also as a mode of perceiving and paying tribute to the wondrous variety of God's creation. Illusion of any kind involves paradox: something is taken for real when, in fact, another thing is the reality. A common form of Renaissance paradox is grounded on a premise of one true, firm, and stable idea existing in a bewildering pluralism of competing apparent truths.[1] There are many paradoxes in Milton's works [2]: the fortunate fall, Christ's descent to light, the blind bard's vision, the principle of freedom in obedience, among others; and the paradoxes of heaven have their counterpart in hell: the self-enslavement of Satan's 'independence', Satan's ascent into darkness, his oblivion gained by glory sought, and the weakness of his 'prowess'. In Milton, many paradoxes stem from the principle of virtue within, and the common phenomenon that the way of the world is often out of touch with the way of the spirit, which results in contrary definitions of such things as freedom, obedience, love, honor, and beauty. In this respect, it is well to remember that all things admit of true and false, before weighing such things as patience and martial valor one against the other. The paradox most often mentioned with respect to Milton's concept of heroic virtue is that God accomplishes "great things, by things deem'd weak", or that highest victory is won by patient suffering; central though this idea is in Milton, it is impossible to ignore another, which the modern mind is less comfortable with – Abdiel's assertion that "he who in debate of truth hath won/ Should win in Arms". For Milton, one is as important as the other; in fact, they go together. I believe that Milton's heroic standard is more Homeric than current interpretation allows.[3]

---

[1]   Rosalie Colie, "Some Paradoxes in the Language of Things", in Joseph Mazzeo, ed., *Reason and the Imagination* (New York, 1962), pp. 109-10.
[2]   Cf. Arthur O. Lovejoy, "Milton and the Paradox of the Fortunate Fall", *ELH*, IV (1937), 161-79; Don Cameron Allen, "Milton and the Descent to Light", *JEGP*, LX, (1961), 614-30; Rosalie Colie, *Paradoxia Epidemica* (Princeton, 1966), pp. 169-89; Anne Ferry, "The Bird, the Blind Bard, and the Fortunate Fall", in Mazzeo, pp. 183-200.
[3]   Milton's idea of heroic virtue has been studied recently by Burton Kurth, *Milton and Christian Heroism* (Berkeley, 1959); Maurice B. McNamee, *Honor and the Epic Hero* (New York, 1960); Douglas Bush, "The Isolation of the Renaissance Hero", in Mazzeo, pp. 57-69; Davis P. Harding, *The Club of Hercules* (Urbana, 1962); Joseph Summers, *The Muse's Method* (London, 1962); Milton Miller, "*Paradise Lost:* the Double Standard", *UTQ*, XX (1951), 183-99; Frank Kermode, "Milton's Hero", *RES* IV n.s. No. 16 (October, 1953), 317-30; John M. Steadman, "The 'Suffering Servant' and Milton's Heroic Norm", *Harvard Theological Review*, LIV

In *Paradise Lost,* Milton developed his heroic perspective by using a number of old literary conventions, conventions which have had a fairly specific meaning in the major epic tradition. This approach is nothing new. In fact, recent space-age studies of metaphoric structures and hidden numerical symbolism make an approach to *Paradise Lost* through the conventions of genre seem old-fashioned and mechanical. Milton's epic conventions have been catalogued for years and by now are a fixture of handbook summaries; as such, they are seemingly an embarrassment to advanced discussions of the poem. The allusions have been traced for added meanings, the sources more or less identified, and the subject put to rest except as a sourcebook for epic details in later literature. We suspect that a poet who uses the local drapery of outworn customs, as Milton did, is bound to suffer trying to adapt them to a new setting, and the epic itself is considered anything but 'organic' in form – an unwieldy framework of conventions valued for its poetic lines and memorable passages, not a sustained and unified performance. If it is but an album of stock responses, it can hardly be a valuable medium which a poet such as Milton could shape to express a grand and subtle theme.

Yet Milton's epic conventions represent a most significant part of the content of the poem. If for no other reason, it is worthwhile to resurrect this literary background *because* it has been considered a dead end. Approaching the epic tradition as though it were a collection of old stage properties guarantees a narrow view of Milton's epics and perhaps cuts us off from insights not to be gained through any other approach except genre. My purpose is not to provide a thorough catalog of conventions, but rather to suggest that some of these conventions are important in defining certain major themes, including his concept of heroic virtue.

In the *Reason of Church Government,* Milton cites Homer, Virgil, and Tasso as models for a 'diffuse' epic, which *Paradise*

(1961), 29-43. Too recent to incorporate here is Steadman's valuable study, *Milton and the Renaissance Hero* (Oxford, 1967).

Lost was to become, and at the same time he talks of laying the 'pattern of a Christian hero'.[4] How Milton used these models has much to do with the heroic pattern which resulted. It is commonly recognized that at the heart of the epic is a pattern of heroic virtue exemplified in the character of the hero. This is no less true of *Paradise Lost*, though sometimes overlooked by studying it exclusively as an argument justifying the ways of God. There is little reason to think that the epic imposes a set of alien values on Milton's subject, significantly modifying what he otherwise would say in a different framework. We cannot regard the epic genre, as we often do the pastoral or the lyric, as a literary exercise whose ideas and commonplaces need not be considered the serious propositions of the poet. The epic was too important to Milton for that; to him, it was the noblest genre, and one which demanded from the poet a special way of life as well as a lifetime of preparation. When he finally put on the singing robes of the epic poet, it was to define what was for him an ideal standard for human conduct as he saw it in the seventeenth century, not to rehearse literary commonplaces.

The pattern of heroic virtue which Milton finally constructed is comprised partly of conventions from the tradition of Homer and Virgil. It is generally agreed by those who value a historical approach at all that to understand a poem in the terms in which it was conceived, the reader needs to know the meaning of the elements that went into its conception. It is useful to know the meaning of these conventions in their earlier sources, for they define Milton's chief characters in formal roles.

Modern interest in the psychology of Milton's characters often threatens to obliterate the sense of their roles, locating 'effects' which are divorced from the ethical pattern to which they belong. But Christ and Satan, Adam and Eve, are well-defined by traditional details and associations which make it possible to determine the role and also the intention of Milton in regard to the role. Satan and Adam are interesting dramatic figures because Milton brings them to life, but he does so within a symbolic

---

[4] *The Works of John Milton*, Columbia Edition (New York, 1931-40), III, 237. This edition is hereafter referred to as "*Works*".

framework, and their psychological motivation is often secondary. Of course, it is important to establish these roles properly. Adam is often taken for the hero of the poem, and, for some readers arouses a sympathy in his plight to the extent that God appears a tyrant and the *felix culpa* ceases to be a paradox. But if Christ, rather than Adam, is the hero of the poem, then a different heroic perspective emerges. Certainly, a correct assessment of the values the poet is celebrating is contingent on a right identification of the hero.

A main contention here is that an awareness of the formal features of Christ's role makes it necessary to question the prevailing view of heroic virtue celebrated in Milton's last works. This view I take to be that Milton sings primarily of patience and 'deeds of peace',[5] and that his thoughts on the essence of heroism are summarized in Book IX, 29-41, where Milton rejects 'hitherto the onely Argument/ Heroic deem'd' ('the deeds of fabl'd Knights/ In Battels feign'd') and chooses instead 'the better fortitude/ Of Patience and Heroic Martyrdom'; and in Book III of *Paradise Regained*, where Christ says that true glory will be attained not by 'ambition, warr, or violence', but by 'deeds of peace, by wisdom eminent,/ By patience, temperance' (88-92). I question the opposition which readers set up between active deeds and patient suffering; for one thing, implicit in this view is a sense of inconsistency or contradiction based on the evidence that Milton's natural inclination in his earlier years was toward the heroic in the traditional epic sense.[6] Thomas Greene views this as a paradox: "The great paradox of *Paradise Lost* lies in Milton's withholding from his human characters that spacious

---

[5] Cf. C. M. Bowra, *From Virgil to Milton* (London, 1945); Northrop Frye, *The Return of Eden* (Toronto, 1965), pp. 23-28; Kurth, pp. 107-34; McNamee, pp. 160-78; Harding, pp. 24-39; Steadman, "The 'Suffering Servant' and Milton's Heroic Norm"; Paul Baumgartner, "Milton and Patience", *SP*, XLX (1963), 203-13; Summers, pp. 122-37.

[6] Baumgartner finds few references to patience in the prose before *De Doctrina* ("in almost every instance Milton mentions patience only to speak of its limitations"), and in the poetry before the sonnet on his blindness (1652-55). He concludes that blindness and adversity changed Milton's mind. "Milton and Patience".

power that ennobled his own imagination."[7] If we view these oft-quoted passages in the epic perspective, however, the great paradox of *Paradise Lost* might be stated in quite another way: the paradox is not that Milton should emerge with a theme that he had ignored for most of his life, but rather that the heroic virtue celebrated in the poem should include some features often noted in Satan. I am not suggesting a return to the Satanist tradition, only that Milton sings of patience and much more.[8]

We shall ignore such formal conventions as the beginning *in medias res* and the use of epic similes to concentrate on certain details of characterization and incident originating in Homer and often derived from ancient customs (e.g. flyting, single combat, the ceremonial council) which are found in the epics of Virgil, Tasso, and Milton. These define Milton's main characters in recognizable epic roles and provide a relatively firm perspective for interpreting them. Milton contrasts Christ and Satan according to a time-honored method of placing different characters in the same situation or role. For example, a wedding is a cultural convention with uniform expectations and well-defined symbols; the character of the bride is supposed to conform to the role which the white dress and veil symbolize – purity and innocence – and when it is well-known that she is otherwise, the symbols may become ironic and traduce the meaning of the ceremony. When something like a bride's veil appears on both Christ and Satan, Milton is not being absent-minded or diabolical, but only aware of the fact that such a convention has subtle possibilities as a literary device. Christ and Satan are introduced in the hero's role on the battlefield, in the council, and on the journey – all

---

[7]   *The Descent from Heaven* (New Haven, 1963), p. 404. McNamee considers it ironic: "It is one of the many ironies of Milton's career that he who dedicated his life to achieving heroic stature himself as the great epic poet should evolve in his epics a concept of the heroic that was nine-tenths a rejection of the heroic motif." p. 175.

[8]   The theme of patience as a feature of Miltonic heroic virtue has been sufficiently stressed elsewhere, and requires no extensive discussion here; in arguing that Milton's heroic perspective also makes room for Homeric elements, and in stressing this martial dimension, I hope that I may safely slight patience without giving the impression that it is unimportant to Milton.

conventions of the epic whose standard meaning enables Milton
to make a subtle and effective contrast according to how they fit
or do not fit the role. Satan the anti-Christ is formally the anti-
hero; not, I think, in order that Milton could make a scholarly
reassessment of the old epic standard, but rather to convey the
sense of paradox in his own concept of heroic virtue.

There is no need at this point to chase the spectre of Satanism,
but the problems which have arisen in modern readings are related. When Christ's heroic virtue is identified with contemplative
humility, and Satan's evil with his dedication to Homeric, warlike
deeds, it has often been noticed that these categories do not fit
very well: the moral gulf between them often seems a rather
narrow margin, and one notices disturbing parallels. It has not
been easy trying to account for this lack of straightforward signs
which would distinguish clearly between the good and evil characters in the poem,[9] and readers who value the poem as a lens
for looking into the mind of Milton seemingly have welcomed
this uncertainty in order to speculate about inner conflicts. But
the fact is that what many have considered scandalously incongruous – that evil should so resemble the good – the Renaissance

---

[9]   See Bowra, pp. 227-34; William Empson, *Some Versions of Pastoral*
(New York, n.d.), pp. 181-85; Malcolm Mackenzie Ross, *Poetry and Dogma*
(New Brunswick, N.J., 1954), pp. 224-25; Milton Miller, "*Paradise Lost:*
the Double Standard"; Other examples: Mark Van Doren's vexation at
seeing Christ as a scornful knight in the very trappings that Milton elsewhere denounces (*The Noble Voice* (New York, 1946), p. 132); J. B. Broadbent's observation that it is anomalous that Christ's chariot should be used
for both creative and destructive purposes (*Some Graver Subject* (London,
1960), pp. 231-32); and John Peter's objection that Milton decorates heaven
with the very materials that he contemptuously dismisses elsewhere as the
livery of gay religion (*A Critique of Paradise Lost* (New York, 1960),
p. 86). R. J. Z. Werblowsky's Jungian exploration is based on a number
of similar observations: "In Book IX, 27-41 Milton scoffs at the chivalric
epic, whilst Michael plays the role of a St. George in a pseudo-Arthurian
heaven. Temples and palaces, symbolizing the contemptibility of earthly
magnificence, are raised in hell by the same architect who had already
previously built them in heaven. Similarly we learn that Mammon, the first
to dig for gold and to propagate the practice, had already had ample
opportunity in heaven to given evidence of his weakness. Apparently gold
and other splendors of heaven should be despised down here as the vanities
of earth." *Lucifer and Prometheus* (London, 1952), p. 10.

considered self-evident. Neither accidental nor incongruous, the parallels define a clear-cut contrast between Christ and Satan.

There are diverse reactions to Adam and Eve to choose from as well, particularly from critics who set to analyze the poem independent of any tradition, judging it in terms of the internal texture presumably observable to any unschooled reader. A. J. A. Waldock assumed that the less we know about the traditions of the poem the better: "Between the impressions of the natural, easy-going, unprejudiced readers, there is, I believe, no great variation. Differences mount with sophistication – because the registering mind, so to say, comes to know too much." [10] Then his own intuitive perception, and that of his disciple John Peter, find that Adam's fall is actually a noble love and courageous sacrifice for Eve [11] – a modernization that suggests a most unique view of the fall. The method of Waldock and Peter imposes some severe and unnecessary limitations; the critic who ignores the tangible guidance that tradition and genre provide, in effect, supposes that he will see better by craning his neck through stocks of his own making.[12]

However one studies *Paradise Lost*, a crucial point of debate has been the mind of Milton. We are sometimes reminded that truth is one thing and art another, that the insights of a literary work are, or ought to be, unrelated to its value as art. The enlightened reader ought therefore to consult the 'organic unity' or formal design of a work rather than its ideas. It is an open question whether such an approach is possible, but even if it were, criticism of *Paradise Lost* falls short of such a goal. In practice, even objective artistic evaluations seem more than a little shaped by moral attitudes in the critic, and our taste for Milton's art is somewhat proportional to our taste for his Puritan morality. It follows that if Milton's moral perspective has been misunderstood

[10] *Paradise Lost and Its Critics* (Cambridge, 1947), p. 26.
[11] *Ibid.*, p. 52; Peter, pp. 150-58.
[12] Bernard Bergonzi points out the incongruity of applying the norms of the novel to the epic. "Criticism and the Milton Controversy", in *The Living Milton*, ed. Frank Kermode (New York, 1961), pp. 162-80; for a general review of contemporary issues, including those raised by Waldock, see Patrick Murray, *Milton: the Modern Phase* (New York, 1967).

– and I think a misunderstanding has been perpetuated in many reassessments – then evaluations of his artistry are also likely to miss the mark. For this reason, the stability which the genre provides should be welcome to the discussion. The reader who knows the epic context of the poem is less likely to find that Christ is a narrow Puritan whose flaming chariot belies his disposition to suffer rather than to do; or that Satan is a villain artistically unsuccessful because dramatically too successful; or that Adam and Eve are lovers whose weakness is rather their strength.

I

MILTON'S EPIC HERO

When Milton's Christ mounts the chariot of wrath to deliver ten thousand thunderbolts in single combat against the rebel legions in Book VI of *Paradise Lost*, it has seemed to many a strange role for the figure whose example teaches Adam that "suffering for Truths sake/ Is fortitude to highest victorie", and whose heroism in *Paradise Regained* exhibits endurance and renunciation instead of active deeds:

> But if there be in glory aught of good,
> It may by means far different be attain'd
> Without ambition, war, or violence;
> By deeds of peace, by wisdom eminent,
> By patience, temperance.   (*P.R.* III, 88-92)[1]

As the angel legions withdraw in silence, one thinks of Achilles ordering his Achaian forces to withdraw so that he alone would have the glory of killing Hector. Christ here seems as much a Homeric warrior as Satan, and the epic paraphernalia thus seems incompatible with the passive virtues which are commonly thought to represent Milton's ideal of heroic virtue: endurance, other-worldliness, humility, and suffering. One of the hazards of reading Milton has been this feeling of uncertainty and contradiction about Christ, as well as the closely associated and more historically interesting puzzle of how to respond to Satan. Given the unequivocal Christian view of Christ and Satan, the anti-Christ, it is unsettling to find similarities between them in a Christian poem.

---

[1] *John Milton: Complete Poems and Major Prose*, ed. Merritt Y. Hughes (New York, 1957). Subsequent references to this edition will appear in the text except where otherwise noted.

For Dryden, a Christian writing an epic faced something of a problem: how to write of heroic actions when the Christian theme required contemplation and suffering:

And 'tis true, that, in the severe notions of our faith, the fortitude of a Christian consists in patience, and suffering, for the love of God, whatever hardships can befall him in the world; not in any great attempt or in performance of these enterprises which the poets call heroic, and which are commonly the effects of interest, ostentation, pride, and worldly honour: that humility and resignation are our prime virtues; and that these include no action, but that of the soul; when as, on the contrary, an heroic poem requires to its necessary design, and as its last perfection, some great extraordinary undertaking; which requires the strength and vigour of the body, the duty of a soldier, and capacity and prudence of a general, and, in short as much or more, of the active virtues, than the suffering.[2]

Several recognized studies have defined Renaissance heroic virtue in broader terms,[3] but Milton's readers still assume an irreconcilable polarity between the claims of Homeric deeds and Christian faith. A common assumption is that Milton was one of those who held 'severe notions' of the Christian faith,[4] and that his concept of heroic virtue is a blend of contemplative humility and patient suffering which has no place for Achillean valor. It is thus tempting to dramatize and exaggerate the difficulty Milton faced in adapting the genre of Homer to a Christian theme, and to assume that he used the great classical models against his better judgment.[5] Following this path, one must envision a poet torn

---

[2] "Original and Progress of Satire", *Essays of John Dryden*, ed. W. P. Ker (Oxford, 1900), II, 30-31.

[3] Merritt Y. Hughes, "The Christ of *Paradise Regained* and the Renaissance Heroic Tradition", *SP*, XXXV (1938), 254-77; Hallett Smith, *Elizabethan Poetry* (Cambridge, Mass., 1952), pp. 290-342. See also A. B. Chambers, "Wisdom and Fortitude in *Samson Agonistes*", *PMLA*, LXXVIII (Sept., 1963), 315-20.

[4] McNamee, for example, emphasizes the element of Stoic withdrawal and ascetic rejection in Milton's idea of heroic virtue, and concludes that this "Stoic and Augustinian coloring in the Miltonic ideal makes the more tolerant view of Spenser stand out with greater clarity." *Honor and the Epic Hero*, p. 175.

[5] Helen Gardner writes that Milton "dared not leave all the active and traditionally heroic virtues to Satan", hence the war in heaven, an anachronism which Milton nevertheless had the virtuosity to include without

between Homer and the Bible, finally effecting a compromise because he was unable to make up his mind – and this, on the greatest project he ever attempted. It is not easy to imagine Milton in this predicament.

There is good reason to believe that this kind of tension between pagan and Christian in the Middle Ages and Renaissance has been overestimated. Instead of seriously challenging medieval faith, the classical heritage occupied a respectable place within the medieval Christian hierarchy. Writers and poets used pagan symbols and ideas with no necessary intention or implication of worldliness or of conflict with the spiritual way of the church. Milton, who is very much in this tradition, freely associates Christ with Hercules, Pan, or Orpheus with no sense of contradiction, and in *Paradise Regained* – supposedly a crux on this point – Christ rejects Satan's offers of classical learning not as such, but because Satan offers a natural learning sufficient unto itself without need of the 'Light from above'.[6] Christ's rebuff is stern because Satan offers wisdom as a means to worldly power and glory; though Milton regarded the classical heritage secondary, he did not consider it irrelevant or hostile to Scriptural truth. Christ says here that though the ancients were without the 'Light from above', they could express moral virtue "By light of

seriously disrupting his theme. *A Reading of Paradise Lost* (Oxford, 1965), pp. 65-71. Thomas Greene notes the difficulty of adapting old conventions to a new subject, "no imported forms can mechanically impose themselves without a sense of artificiality". He finds no such mechanical imposition with respect to the celestial descent – the single convention he studies ("the only epic to incorporate the celestial descent into a larger ... comprehensive pattern of imagery"); only with respect to those he notes in passing does he find discrepancies: an "admiration for angelic prowess and yet contempt for human military prowess", and a characterization of Adam in the last books which contained "the seeds of the genre's destruction" because it lacks the energy of traditional heroism. *The Descent from Heaven*, pp. 403-18.

[6] C. A. Patrides remarks, "... Jesus utters a commonplace of Christian thought: that after the Fall the *lex naturae* is almost always an 'imperfect illumination,' an uncertain guide likely to mislead us unless we take the further step in the direction of 'those writt'n Records pure'." *Milton and the Christian Tradition* (Oxford, 1966), p. 86; see also Barbara Lewalski, *Milton's Brief Epic* (Providence, 1966), pp. 281-91.

Nature, not in all quite lost" (*P.R.* IV, 351-52), consistent, it will be remembered, with his view in *Of Education* that reading the ancients has a moral as well as a practical purpose. How important this heritage is to the life of the spirit is seen in *Areopagitica*: Milton cites Julian the Apostate as the most dangerous enemy of the Christian faith because he isolated the Christians from pagan learning and caused their faith to wither away in ignorance.[7]

Nor do the martial norms of the epic genre necessarily conflict with the canons of Milton's immediate Christian background. In seeking a suitable model for his conception of heroic virtue in Christ, Milton had more to choose from than the suffering servant of Isaiah's prophecy.[8] Close at hand, and certainly a part of his own experience, was the Puritan saga of the wayfaring and warfaring soul dramatized by seventeenth-century Puritan preachers. William Haller has described, in the dominant themes of these contemporary sermons, a militant virtue decidedly heroic. The sermons were full of epic-sounding allusions to spiritual wayfaring and warfaring, and often called forth the image of a Puritan soldier pressed into battle in the unceasing wars of the spiritual against the carnal man.[9] It seems likely that such a background is present in Milton's two epics, for Christ the suffering servant is modified considerably by features of the warrior-king David. For perhaps the same reasons, Milton's own program in *Of Education* for schooling the young in Christian virtue is more than a little Homeric in its preparation for warfaring:

The exercise which I commend first is the exact use of their weapon, to guard and to strike safely with edge or point; this will keep them healthy, nimble, strong, and well in breath – is also the likeliest means to make them grow large and tall, and to inspire them with a gallant

[7] "So great an injury they then held it to be deprived of Hellenic learning; and thought it a persecution more undermining and secretly decaying the Church, than the open cruelty of Decius or Diocletian." Hughes, *Complete Poems and Major Prose*, p. 726.
[8] John M. Steadman, "The 'Suffering Servant' and Milton's Heroic Norm", *Harvard Theological Review*, LIV (Jan., 1961), 29-43, confines his examination of Christ to the tradition of the suffering servant.
[9] *The Rise of Puritanism* (New York, 1957), p. 142.

and fearless courage, which, being tempered with seasonable lectures and precepts to them of true fortitude and patience, will turn into a native and heroic valor, and make them hate the cowardice of doing wrong.

We look to the epic hero for the highest values of the poet and his culture – to Achilles for primitive Greek ideals, to Aeneas for the highest values of Augustan Rome, and to Godfredo and Arthur for the ideals of Christian chivalry. It is thus important to have the hero straight; the reader who looks for heroic virtue in Agamemnon or Turnus works with faulty models and will emerge with a distorted perspective. The notion that Satan is the hero is largely discredited, but it is still possible to interpret Miltonic heroic virtue on the assumption that Adam is the hero, despite the fact that Adam's fall can hardly be considered an epic action at all. Adam, whose response to temptation is a failure of heroic virtue, fits rather a tragic pattern, at odds with the motive of the epic. When assessing Michael's admonition to Adam to exhibit humility, it is helpful to remember that the latter had recently displayed a world-shaking pride.

Nor is the problem simplified by considering the poem a tragedy. *Paradise Lost* may have started out to be a dramatic tragedy, as the Cambridge manuscript indicates, but it is basically an epic, and we must look for heroic virtue in Christ, the only victorious figure in the poem. A substantial Christian tradition considered Christ the model of heroic virtue, and Milton is no innovator in this respect. In Book XII, Milton balances his account of Adam's loss with an account of the Redemption, and characterizes the coming of Christ in traditional heroic terms:

> A Virgin is his Mother, but his Sire
> The Power of the most High; he shall ascend
> The Throne hereditarie, and bound his Reign
> With earth's wide bounds, his glory with the Heav'ns.
>   (XII, 368-71)

C. A. Patrides emphasizes the extent to which Christ "renders coherence to the entire epic":

The role of protagonist, once assigned to him, is maintained in all subsequent events. As Creator he erects the universal edifice (VII, 210 ff.);

as Saviour he volunteers to redeem man long before the Fall (III, 236 ff.); as Judge he passes sentence on Adam and Eve (X, 97 ff.); through his Prevenient Grace he is instrumental in their regeneration (XI, 2 ff.); as the incarnate Christ he consummates the salvation for which he had earlier offered himself (III, 236 ff., XII, 360 ff); through his Comforter he supports his faithful followers (XII, 485 ff.); and as the Supreme Judge he is to return in order to terminate the history of the world.[10]

Adam is a central figure, but the genre itself provides the most conclusive evidence that Christ is the formal hero, for Milton, in both *Paradise Lost* and *Paradise Regained,* presents Christ with traditional features associated with the hero's role in heroic poetry. It will thus be useful in this chapter to look at *Paradise Regained* as well. Though the occasion in *Paradise Regained* focuses naturally on renunciation, there is no contradiction between the patient figure on the desert who reminds Satan, "Yet he who reigns within himself, and rules/ Passions, Desires, and Fears, is more a King" (II, 466-67), and the towering warrior in the war in heaven.

Of course, there are no ready-made Christian heroes in Homer: many values in Homer were incompatible with the Christian ethic, and consequently many changes took place when epics were written by Christians. Nevertheless, many Homeric elements passed into Christian epics and became important means of defining the Christian subject. A brief survey of certain important changes from classical to Christian epics will suggest how certain Homeric conventions ultimately contributed to a complex pattern of heroic virtue in Milton's Christ.[11]

The Trojan War was anything but a crusade in Europe. Helen is an unmatchable beauty, but for the Greek and Trojan heroes not worth the struggle and sacrifice. Achilles himself laments that the Greeks "now in a strange land make war upon the Trojans

[10]   *Milton and the Christian Tradition*, pp. 260-61.
[11]   Many of the more significant aspects of the change from Homeric to Christian heroism have been thoroughly examined and are now commonplace. I am particularly indebted to Bowra, *From Virgil to Milton*, McNamee, Hallett Smith, Hughes, "The Christ of *Paradise Regained* . . ." and C. S. Lewis, *A Preface to Paradise Lost* (London, 1942).

for the sake of accursed Helen" (*Iliad* XIX, 325-26).[12] That they struggle over what amounts to a trifle is certainly evident to Odysseus, turned into an alien wanderer, away from his wife and son, and to Hector who loses everything for the sake of a brother he comes to scorn. In fact, Paris, who is found on Helen's couch instead of the battlefield, brings to focus the irony of this unworthy quest in his own casual behavior.[13] What makes this dubious quest worthy to these Homeric warriors is Honor. In a later age, Hamlet defines what it was that made the Greek expedition worthwhile: "Rightly to be great/ Is not to stir without great argument/ But greatly to find quarrel in a straw/ When honor's at the stake" (IV, iv). The tragic waste of the expedition against Troy even accentuates the nobility of the Homeric hero who fights for an intangible reward. The cause itself is unimportant when the highest experience in life is a single combat of two heroes. We are thus able to understand why Sarpedon should come from far-away Lykia to fight alongside Hector when he has no quarrel with the Greeks (*Iliad* V, 480-84). Or why Hector and Ajax should engage in a pitched battle in a style marked by considerable formal ceremony, even to exchanging gifts. They battle not out of rancor, but for the sake of honor, and this bond sets them apart from ordinary men.

In the main action of the *Iliad*, it is honor which sidetracks the Greek expedition. Achilles is truly the magnanimous hero, as Aristotle defined magnanimity – the rational attitude of a genuinely great man (great because pre-eminent in the practice of all

[12]   All citations from the *Iliad* will be from the translation of Richmond Lattimore, *The Iliad of Homer* (Chicago, 1951). Reprinted by permission of the University of Chicago Press. Copyright 1951 by The University of Chicago. All citations from the *Odyssey* will be from the translation of T. E. Shaw, *The Odyssey of Homer* (New York, 1956). Reprinted by permission of the Oxford University Press.
[13]   *Iliad* III, 30-45, 428-46. McNamee sees Paris' counterpart, Menelaus, in the same way. "He is mediocre in almost every respect, but is forever volunteering or eager and ambitious to take up challenges that are beyond his capacities. ... He has to be frequently reminded of his limitations and gently shown his place even by his brother Agamemnon. But his mediocrity is a foil against which Achilles' superiority shines the brighter." pp. 12, 33-34.

the virtues honored in the culture) toward his own personal honor. He demands and receives the honor that he deserves by virtue of his excellence, and he is extremely jealous of that honor in battle. Achilles withdraws from the field because Agamemnon has dishonored him by claiming Briseis (XVI, 56-59). Given the premise of Honor, Achilles' revenge upon Agamemnon is justified,[14] even though his wrath imperils the entire Greek force. In the *Odyssey* Agamemnon himself testifies to Achilles' complete success in winning glory, and clearly envies him his hero's funeral (XXIV, pp. 314-16). Thus Achilles' self-centered search for Honor is presented not as a dubious or a dangerous quality but as a high and noble aim for which he must sacrifice all that ordinary men hold dear. In their primitive context, Achilles' values are lofty and intangible. He must make the classic choice between a short life with honor and a long life of obscure domestic bliss; he must sacrifice the tangible rewards of heroism for the intangible. The nature of the Greek quest is unimportant and even provides an ironic counterpoint to accentuate the stature of the brave warriors who fight in a poor cause. Achilles is the standard by which the others, namely Agamemnon, are judged: he scorns Agamemnon's hopes of winning wealth and spoil, "O wrapped in shamelessness, with your mind forever on profit, how shall any one of the Achaians readily obey you either to go on a journey or to fight men strongly in battle?" (*Iliad* I, 149-51).

If the *Iliad* sings of warfare and glory of Achilles, the *Odyssey* sings of wandering and the resourcefulness and subtlety of Odysseus.[15] In the *Iliad*, his wisdom unites the Achaians; in the *Odyssey*, his intelligence enables him to survive the long journey

---

[14] There are as many interpretations of the *Iliad* as there have been of *Paradise Lost*. Many consider Achilles a tragic figure (Cf. Lattimore, pp. 44-48; L. A. Post, *From Homer to Menander* (Berkeley, 1951); C. M. Bowra, *Tradition and Design in the Iliad* (Oxford, 1930)), but I interpret him as do McNamee (pp. 1-39) and Cedric Whitman, *Homer and the Heroic Tradition* (Cambridge, 1958), as the successful epic hero and heroic standard of the poem.
[15] The subtlety and eloquence of Odysseus and Nestor were as prized as the valor of Achilles. Ernst Robert Curtius, *European Literature and the Latin Middle Ages*, trans. Willard Trask (London, 1953), p. 172.

home. Yet another important theme of the *Odyssey* involves neither the battlefield where the hero's honor is won, nor the desolate journey where the wandering hero's character is tested, but rather the home where the dignities earned on the battlefield are reflected in the social code and the ceremonial exercise of hospitality. Telemachus is young and vulnerable because his father's fate is unknown, and he is neither strong nor experienced enough to control the suitors in his father's house. He is unable to assume his father's role in exercising the proper ceremony and hospitality of the lord of the house.[16] Consequently, without the strength and stature of his father, Telemachus is, to begin with, forced into quite another role, in Homer decidedly unheroic; he can only endure with the weak (*Odyssey* III, p. 34).

These particular elements in Homer's characterization of epic heroism underwent interesting modifications in Virgil's *Aeneid*. If the expedition to burn Troy in the *Iliad* is a dubious one (the Greek leaders themselves were loath to honor their pledge to Menelaus), the quest for a new Troy in the *Aeneid* is the very heart of the story. Aeneas' quest is a lofty goal which he cannot reach until he becomes worthy of it. He must achieve a heroic virtue which encompasses the highest values of Augustan Rome before he can become its founder.[17] And so Aeneas is not a proven hero but rather an untried leader who must pass the test. Moreover, Roman heroic virtue valued not a self-centered heroism and pursuit of honor, but rather duty and dedication to the aims of the state. In this new light, Virgil re-interpreted Achilles' noble wrath as mere cruelty, and Odysseus' cleverness as treachery.[18]

---

[16]   *Odyssey* XVI, p. 223. The importance of the practice of hospitality as a motif is seen in the elaborate hospitality of Menelaus (IV, pp. 44-45) and Alcinous (VII, pp. 98-99), in the abuse of hospitality by Cyclops (IX, pp. 123-33), in the account of the death of Agamemnon (XI, p. 163), and when Odysseus is abused in his own hall (XVII, pp. 242-43); finally, in the gracious hospitality of the humble but faithful servant, Eumeus (XV, p. 217).

[17]   I am particularly indebted in this section to Bowra, pp. 33-85 and McNamee, pp. 51-74.

[18]   Cf. *Aeneid* II, 29, 43-44. All citations from the *Aeneid* will be from the translation of J. W. Mackail, *Virgil's Works* (New York, 1950). Reprinted by permission of Random House, Inc.

And Neoptolemus, Achilles' son, changes from hero to villain; his deeds greatly honor his dead father in the *Odyssey* (XI, pp. 165-66), but he emerges in the *Aeneid* as a degenerate and brutal murderer, attacking the helpless household of Priam (II, 499-558). As for martial glory, Virgil conveys a sense of sadness in defeat, and emphasizes the horror and tragic waste of battlefield slaughter rather than the great feats of warriors. Aeneas' heroic efforts consist often of restraint and endurance. He is told that "all fortune may be overcome by being borne" (V, 710), and he learns that honor can also be won by enduring defeat and ruin (I, 461-63). Aeneas feels the anger of vengeance and is aware how noble it is to die in battle, but he feels more heavily the responsibility he has for the future, and he seeks instead the safety of his family (II, 316-17, 707-11). As C. M. Bowra has pointed out, Aeneas' virtue is built on a Stoic plan, wherein the life of virtue was seen as a warfare filled with hardships and temptations.[19] The hero becomes wise through *exercitatio*, a vigorous and continual test demanding duty, prudence, self-control, and endurance.

Yet Virgil does not ignore the martial virtues. His hero of wisdom and temperance thunders forth in battle with all the wrath and might of Achilles:

> Sweeping terrible down the tide of battle
> he wakens fierce indiscriminate carnage,
> and flings loose all the reins of wrath.
>
> (*Aeneid* XII, 497-99)

The dramatic single combat of Turnus and Aeneas is very much in the tradition of Hector and Achilles. In effect, Aeneas endures misfortune and gains in virtue with the exercise of his prudence and self-discipline and then proves his mastery in battle. This becomes a fundamental pattern in Christian epics. Aeneas has none of Achilles' zeal for bloodshed, but when the occasion becomes necessary, he becomes a Homeric warrior, and with no mixed feelings. In brief, as his introduction to Dido indicates, Aeneas is both a righteous man and a warrior, "Aeneas was our

[19]   *From Virgil to Milton*, p. 59.

king, foremost of men in righteousness, incomparable in goodness, as in warlike arms" (I, 544-45).

Christian poets found Aeneas a very good model for certain
features of Christian heroic virtue, in particular the fine balance
between self-discipline and martial valor. Instead of duty to
Rome, however, the basic principles of heroic virtue in Christian
epics are expressed in the two great commandments:

Thou shalt love the Lord thy God with all thy heart and with all thy
soul, and with all thy mind. This is the first and great commandment.
And the second is like unto it; Thou shalt love thy neighbor as thyself.
On these two commandments hang all the Law and the Prophets.

All other qualities of heroic virtue stem from obedience to God
and the charity which is inseparable from it. Since all things are
of God, who embodies the highest value, the single highest good
is keeping the bond with God. Thus obedience is the keystone,
and it gives substance to love and wisdom,[20] but these expressions
of the human spirit are difficult to separate in this way, for love
is an all-embracing concept based on the example of the free gift
of Grace manifested by God toward man in the person of Christ,[21]
and wisdom is nothing less than knowing God aright. Obeying
God means loving God in imitation of God's love, and it also
means knowing God. Despite the apparent simplicity of these
commandments, the Christian faces a bewildering variety of
wrong choices, all subtly testing his moral discernment − his
ability to maintain his commitment to these commands. The
Christian poet translated Virgil's ideal of loyalty to the state into
obedience to God, and gave the Christian hero a more complex

[20] "Virtue is being allied to the source of goodness; happiness is the
psychological peace of being allied to the source of goodness (this will
serve for innocence also); heroism is choosing to remain allied to the source
of goodness; knowledge and wisdom are the recognition of the source of
goodness." Stanley E. Fish, *Surprised by Sin* (New York, 1967), p. 333.
Arnold Stein places knowledge at the apex instead of obedience. *Heroic
Knowledge* (Minneapolis, 1957), pp. 17-35.
[21] For an excellent discussion of the central place of Grace, and the
troublesome issue it raised for everyone, including Milton, of the relation
between the premise of free will and the equally compelling premise of
Grace as an unmerited gift, see Patrides, pp. 187-219.

choice than that which faced Aeneas.[22] It is more difficult (as the subtle temptations of *Paradise Regained* make clear) for the Christian hero to know what the higher destiny is, hence difficult to keep his eye firmly on it.

As for the glory of Achilles, Saint Paul gave the Christian reply, "But he that glorieth, let him glory in the Lord", and Saint Thomas defined it at length:

Honour denotes reverence shown to a person in witness of his excellence. Now two things have to be considered with regard to man's honour. The first is that a man has not from himself the thing in which he excels, for this is, as it were, something Divine in him, wherefore on this count honour is due principally, not to him but to God. The second point that calls for observation is that the thing in which man excels is given to him by God, that he may profit others thereby; wherefore a man ought so far to be pleased that others bear witness to his excellence, as this enables him to profit others.[23]

Honor must be subordinate to dependence and charity: "Now the desire for honor may be inordinate in three ways. First, when a man desires recognition of an excellence which he has not. . . . Secondly, when a man desires honor himself without referring it to God. Thirdly, when man's appetite rests in honor itself, without referring it to the profit of others." [24] This does not rule out earthly honors themselves: if a man seeks first the glory of God and makes his excellence serve the ends of charity, then the earthly rewards and honors that accrue to him (incidentally, and as a consequence of his dependence and charity) will be entirely appropriate. To a certain degree in the Christian tradition, there was also a tendency to equate worldly honor with godlessness, as though the extent to which a man obtained honor was the extent to which he departed from the life of the spirit – a rigorous application implied in the *contemptus mundi* theme, and sometimes in the lesson of the falls of princes. It has also been attributed to Milton, seemingly on the premise that as a Puritan he ought to

[22] Douglas Knight suggests that suffering in Aeneas is the result of submitting himself to his destiny, whereas in a Christian epic, man suffers because he "cannot adequately discipline the privileges he is unable to renounce". *Pope and the Heroic Tradition* (New Haven, 1951), pp. 88-89.
[23] *Summa Theologica*, trans. Fathers of the English Dominican Province, II (New York, 1947), IIa, IIae, Q. 131, Art. I, p. 1737.
[24] *Ibid.*

have an otherworldly cast, but there is little in *Paradise Lost* or *Paradise Regained* to support it.

The Christian tradition also applied the heroic test demanded of Aeneas that the hero exhibit reason and temperance against great odds. The Renaissance hero fought his most difficult battles in overcoming himself, and accordingly, his adventures were designed to show his prudence and self-control. Since virtue was not a moment of insight but a long and difficult path, the Christian hero was wayfaring as well as warfaring, and along a road every bit as difficult as the old road to heroic glory. He had much the same choice too – either the easy way to pleasure and worldly rewards, or the strenuous road to God. (The way to hell was always easy, the way back, difficult). Consequently, the epic test in the Christian tradition demanded fortitude and endurance. The chorus in *Samson Agonistes* surveys the situation of fallen Samson and concludes that instead of doing great deeds, he must join the lot of those "Whom Patience finally must crown". Milton praises the 'better fortitude/ Of Patience and Heroic Martyrdom', and Chapman's Ulysses demonstrates his ability to endure patiently all that the gods have in store for him. To the sixteenth century, Hercules was a moral hero, a model of restraint and prudence, admired as much for his self-discipline as for his exploits. Aeneas too was an inevitable model for heroic virtue, having become in the Middle Ages symbolic of the pilgrimage of Everyman toward his destined home in the eternal city of God. And one of the likeliest models for Christian heroism was Job, whose long suffering taught him the lessons the Christian hero must know. Since earthly honors and rewards are only incidental and unimportant, the Christian hero, if he endures, receives, in God's own good time, his true honors in heaven.

These features of heroic virtue are exemplified in the Christian epics as far back as *Beowulf*. Hrothgar warns Beowulf that his great strength must serve God, who has granted him glory and wealth, and will take it away (1724-70).[25] He cites a certain

---

[25] Hrothgar's sermon on pride. All citations from *Beowulf* are from the translation of Charles W. Kennedy, *Beowulf* (New York, 1940). Reprinted by permission of The Oxford University Press.

princely ruler who, in his 'fullness of worldly joy', becomes
proud. Forgetting a proper dependence on God, he then "has no
defense for the fierce assaults/ Of the loathsome Fiend", and
finally considers himself a self-made man. He forgets his spiritual
end only to learn the bitter lesson not to lay up treasure on earth
where thieves break through and steal, "Death descends, and another seizes/ His hoarded riches and rashly spends/ The princely
treasure" (1755-57). Hrothgar's lesson to Beowulf is "Avoid such
evil and seek the good,/ The heavenly wisdom. Beware of pride."
Tasso's *Jerusalem Delivered* is, in one sense, an elaborate allegory
of the lesson of Hrothgar's sermon. Godfredo, the Christian leader
and symbol of reason, has a task worthy of Aeneas, "The Christian folk from bondage to have brought,/ Wherein, alas, they
long have lived thrall" (I, xxiii).[26] Most of the action portrays the
extended preparations of the Christian knights to become worthy
of this quest; they can capture the holy city only after they exhibit
the temperance and self-mastery of Christian virtue. Godfredo's
aims accord with several chief features of Christian heroic virtue.
They seek no glory or the conquest of new lands, but only a
heavenly reward and the ends of God (I, xxii; lxxxii). Nor has
their success been their own; they conquer by "heav'ns mere
grace, not by . . . prowess done". Their power is not derived from
spear and shield, but from God (I, xxii), and it will be withdrawn
if they swerve from their high purpose.

This sense of Christian purpose is as strong in Spenser's
knights as it is in Godfredo. Indeed, it is axiomatic that a knight's
actions can only be judged by their 'end', by their inner spiritual
purpose:

> Yet gold al is not, that doth golden seeme,
> Ne all good knights, that shake well speare and shield:
> The worth of all men by their end esteeme,
> And then dew praise or dew reproch them yield.
>
> (*Faerie Queene* II, viii, 14)[27]

---

[23]   All citations from *Jerusalem Delivered* are from the sixteenth-century
translation of Edward Fairfax (London, 1890).
[27]   All citations from the *Faerie Queene* are from *The Complete Poetical
Works of Spenser*, ed. R. E. Neil Dodge (Boston, 1936).

Arthur seeks the heavenly perfection of Queen Gloriana, Redcrosse knight climbs the ladder of perfection toward holiness,
and Guyon proves his temperance by overcoming the temptress,
Acrasia. In each case the end of the quest is reached when the
hero proves his heroic virtue by overcoming temptation. Guyon
is tempted right and left before he purges Acrasia's bower, and
Redcrosse's pilgrimage tests not his battle prowess so much as
his reason and self-discipline. In orthodox fashion, Spenser's
knights seek only God's glory, and their strength is His. Gloriana,
whom Arthur and Redcrosse serve, is not Homeric but Thomistic.
Spenser distinguishes between the true heavenly glory and the
false earthly glory of Philotime, and defines true virtue as a
proper dependence:

> What man is he, that boasts of fleshly might,
> And vaine assurance of mortality,
> Which, all so soone as it doth come to fight
> Against spirituall foes, yields by and by,
> Or from the fielde most cowardly doth fly?
> Ne let the man ascribe it to his skill,
> That thorough grace hath gained victory
> If any strength we have, it is to ill,
> But all the good is God's, both power and eke will.
>
> (I, x, 1)

There is no essential difference when we turn to Milton. The
same dependence and charity are found in Christ, whose first and
most important act of heroism is the atonement. In the heavenly
council, God asks "Dwells in all Heaven charity so dear?" (*P.L.*
III, 216). Christ's charity means nothing less than sacrificing his
position of honor at the right hand of God (III, 238-40). This
does not in itself imply an attitude of Stoic withdrawal, for it
should be clear that the Son of God is honored in heaven not for
his voluntary abasement – the renunciation of glory is ancillary –
but for his charity: "O unexampl'd love,/ Love nowhere to be
found less than Divine!" (III, 410-11). Milton's idea of glory, in
fact, seems much like Spenser's. The true glory which Christ
gains in *Paradise Lost*, he defines in *Paradise Regained*:

> This is true glory and renown, when God
> Looking on th' Earth, with approbation marks

> The just man, and divulges him through Heaven
> To all his Angels, who with true applause
> Recount his praises.   (*P.R.* III, 60-64)

God may well honor him who honors God, "Yet so much bounty is in God, such grace,/ That who advance his glory, not thir own,/ Them he himself to glory will advance." (*P.R.* III, 141-44).

Paradise Regained is essentially an account of Christ's 'firm obedience fully tried'. Christ replies to every one of Satan's persuasive arguments with a firm and unwavering assertion of the first commandment: "It is written/ The first of all Commandments, Thou shalt worship/ The Lord thy God, and only him shalt serve" (*P.R.* IV, 175-77). Christ will assume only the kingdom which God intends, and only when God intends it (III, 182-83). In *Paradise Lost* Christ enters the war in heaven sustained by a virtue and grace bestowed by God (VI, 703-04); he knows that he is only God's agent, carrying out what God has ordained and given him the power to do, and that the honor is due to God alone (VI, 723-32). In brief, Milton's hero, no less than Tasso's or Spenser's, exemplifies obedience and charity, and his success depends upon the extent to which these virtues shape his quest. Hence the Christian quest is not counterpointed against the hero's nobler aspirations, nor is it otherwise incidental; it is central to heroic virtue itself. The Christian hero could be truly heroic only if his quest were truly worthy; at the same time, following the pattern of Aeneas, he could achieve his goal only when he himself had become worthy of it. Godfredo, Guyon, Arthur, and Christ all prove their worth by exercising their reason, by resisting temptation, and by patiently enduring all tribulation.

The Bible offers, however, the story of David's victory over Goliath as well as Job's patience as models for epic heroism, and Renaissance poets valued one as well as the other. Thomas Rymer criticized Cowley's second-rate epic, *Davideis*, because it presented only a theme of suffering,[28] and Renaissance critics

---

[28] *Monsieur Rapin's Reflections on Aristotle's Treatise of Poesie* (London, 1694), sigs. B₁-B₂v. As quoted in H. T. Swedenberg, Jr., *The Theory of the Epic in England 1650-1800* (Berkeley, 1944), p. 48.

generally assumed that martial deeds were the proper subject for
the epic. Mazzoni defined heroic poetry as a genre whose audience were chiefly soldiers,[29] and Robortelli, Giraldi, Scaliger, and
Castelvetro agreed that kings and magnanimous men of arms
were the appropriate characters for a genre which dealt with
wars, councils and magnificent actions.[30] We find the same interest in martial deeds in the epics of Tasso and Spenser, who
present their patient, enduring heroes also in the role of avenger
and destroyer. Godfredo's quest in *Jerusalem Delivered* is a siege
modeled on the action of the *Iliad*. Rinaldo, 'brave, as was the
son of Peleus old' (III, xxxviii), and the greatest warrior on either
side, angrily withdraws from the field. He is as indispensable to
the Christians as Achilles was to the Greeks; they cannot win
until he returns. His relation to Godfredo is, in fact, symbolic of
Christian heroic virtue. Hugo tells Godfredo "Thou art this
army's head, and he the hand:/ No other champion can his place
supply" (XIV, xiii). As in the *Song of Roland* ("Roland est
preux, et Olivier est sage"), Tasso uses two figures to make up
one hero: the reason and prudence of Godfredo must be sup-
plemented by the martial valor of Rinaldo, and the implication
is clear that the complete Christian hero is a blend of contemplative wisdom and martial valor.

There is little doubt of Spenser's part in this martial tradition.
He invokes the Muse to help him sing of 'trumpets stern', and,
as a matter of course, his Christian knights have the martial
virtues. The reason that Spenser and other Christian poets valued
the active virtues of Achilles perhaps can be found in Spenser's
portrayal of the quest of Calidore, who forsakes the active life
and his quest in order to enjoy a life of pastoral innocence with
Pastorella. Having put down his arms, he has nothing but a
shepherd's hook (VI, x, 36), which leaves him ill-equipped in a

---

[29] *On the Defense of the Comedy of Dante*, in Allan H. Gilbert, *Literary
Criticism: Plato to Dryden* (New York, 1940), p. 382; See also Sidney's
remark that "Orlando Furioso or honest King Arthur will never displease
a soldier", in Gilbert, p. 442.
[30] Ralph C. Williams, "The Purpose of Poetry, and Particularly the Epic,
as Discussed by Critical Writers of the Sixteenth Century in Italy", *The
Romanic Review*, XII (1921), pp. 7, 13, 17.

world inhabited by brigands and the Blatant Beast. Calidore
would pursue the contemplative ideal in the pastoral setting, but
the fallen world will not support such a life. Thus he must put on
his armor again, first to rescue Pastorella from robbers, and then
to subdue the Blatant Beast. This is perhaps why Belphoebe
earlier has reminded Braggadochio that "deeds of armes and
prowesse martiall!/ All virtue merits praise, but such the most
of all" (II, iii, 37).

This is perhaps sufficient background to see why Milton's God
summons Christ to battle in *Paradise Lost* with 'Bow and Thunder', and tells him "my Almighty Arms/ Gird on, and Sword
upon thy puissant thigh". The other angels stand back in silence
and awe as Christ, in single combat against the enemy, becomes
a figure of terror and wrath. He returns from his victory in glory,
'With Jubilee advanc'd', accompanied by angel legions singing his
triumph and praising his great feat (VI, 882-87). At the end of
Paradise Regained, the angels warn Satan of the kind of foe he
faces, "hereafter learn with awe/ To dread the Son of God". A
closer look at the martial conventions themselves will give a
clearer understanding of the heroic virtue they help define.

The epic hero was very often an untested, or sometimes an
unworthy son. One of the interesting features of Beowulf's background is the hint that he seemed an unworthy son in his youth: [31]

> He had long been scorned, when the sons of the Geats
> Accounted him worthless; the Weder lord
> Held him not high among heroes in hall.
> Laggard they deemed him, slothful and slack.
> But time brought solace for all his ills!   (2183-87)

Achilles too had come away from Greece without completing the
ceremonies for assuming his manhood, emerging from obscurity
to prove himself. The same motif is found in the characterization
of Aeneas in the *Iliad*: he is found by Deiphobos at the "utter-
most edge of the battle, standing, since he was forever angry with
brilliant Priam/ because great as he was, he did him no honour

[31]   Kennedy points out that some of the analogues to *Beowulf* in Icelandic
and Scandinavian myth also present a hero who is little esteemed in his
youth, pp. xxii-xxiii. It is also true of the untested knights of King Arthur,
Spenser's Redcrosse, and Tasso's Rinaldo.

among his people" (XIII, 459-61). Virgil continues the motif in the *Aeneid*. Aeneas is untested and obscure, a hero whose fame is known only to the gods. Homer's Telemachus is not only obscure and untested, but also little esteemed. The suitors scorn him in the assembly because his merit does not match his birthright; there is nothing left for him to do but set forth in exile, later to return a figure to be reckoned with.[32]

Such a convention also indicates that the hero's lineage is important. The common formula referring to the 'son of Ecgtheow' or 'Peleus' son' suggests not only that the poet used an oral technique but also that he attached some meaning to lineage. Iris, urging Achilles to revenge Patroclus, reminds him of his father's honor, "Rise up, Son of Peleus', and Odysseus speaks to him in the same terms: "surely thus your father Peleus advised you/ that day when he sent you away to Agamemnon ... keep from the bad complication of quarrel" (*Iliad* IX, 252-57). Achilles' own son, Neoptolemus, honors his great name, which is what Aeneas has in mind when he urges Ascanius, "as thou recallest the pattern of thy kindred, let thy father Aeneas, thine uncle Hector arouse thy courage" (*Aeneid* XII, 438-40). Young Telemachus, on the other hand, feels unequal to the honor of the great name he bears and wishes that he were the son of an ordinary man. Athene admonishes him: "I think when Penelope conceived so goodly a son it was meant that the Gods had not appointed a nameless future for your stock" (*Odyssey* I, p. 7). When he comes of age, both he and Odysseus think in terms of lineage:

> "My Telemachus, you are taking part with men in battle
> where the best will win. Learn instantly not to disgrace
> your lineage: ours has had a world-reputation for courage
> and skill" – and to this Telemachus replied – "you will
> see me in such form as will indeed not disgrace my forbears."
> (XXIV, p. 326)

[32] Albert Lord associates Telemachus with certain common motifs in Yugoslavian epics in which the young hero is often thought a weakling, is often fatherless, and must borrow the means of transportation when he sets out to prove himself. *The Singer of Tales* (Cambridge, Mass, 1960), pp. 161-63.

The hero must think of his son as well as his father. Mercury reminds Aeneas that he lingers in the arms of Dido when he should be thinking of his son (IV, 271-75), and the appeal is not lost upon the Roman hero who dreams of the wrong done to Ascanius "in cheating him of an Hesperian kingdom and destined fields" (IV, 351-55). The most fortunate son was Achilles', assured of an honorable birthright by the glorious fate of his father. Less fortunate was Orestes, whose father was ignobly murdered in his own house. In Hades, Achilles laments Agamemnon's unfortunate end, for it can only mean an ignoble fate instead of great glory for Orestes. Telemachus' predicament is much like Orestes', for the fate of Odysseus is unknown. If Odysseus had died like Achilles, "the fellowship of Greece would have united to rear his funerary mound and the fame of his prowess would have been a glorious and increasing heritage" (*Odyssey* I, p. 7). But the uncertain fate of his father leaves Telemachus without his birthright and the protection of his father's honor. The same motif is seen in the pathetic vision of Andromache who sees in Hector's death her son, Astyanax, turned into an outcast. (*Iliad* XXII, 487-98).

Achilles' statement indicates that considerable significance was attached to another martial convention – the funeral ceremonies accorded the hero who died in battle. In the classical epic, the funeral signified that the warrior hero had achieved glory and a measure of immortality in a world which offered only the prospect of ultimate death. The elaborate ceremonies which honored Achilles expressed the immortality which he gained: the Achaians kept up a furious battle defending his body; they built a funeral pyre; they "piled a great tomb that towers on its jutting headland far over the Hellespont, a mark for seafaring men of . . . days to come"; the nine Muses joined in the funeral dirge; and the Achaians conducted funeral games after the ceremonies. As a result, Achilles' death has not robbed him of his name, for "everywhere and forever . . . [he] will inherit glory" (*Odyssey* XXIV, pp. 314-16). This pattern is repeated in other great funerals, that of Beowulf,[33] Patroclus (*Iliad* XXIII, 1-225), and

---

[33] For Beowulf, a great pyre is built, a mournful dirge is sung over the body, and a barrow is erected on a headland in order to be visible to sea-

Pallas (*Aeneid* XI, 1-202). This is why it was customary to fight
over the body of the dead hero. The alternative to a ceremonial
burial was to lie unburied on the field, the prey to dogs and
ravens – an ignoble fate which Hector feared above all else
(*Iliad* VII, 76-79; XXII, 338-43), for it meant only dishonor and
oblivion. Agamemnon tells us that this was the fate reserved for
cowards:

> But any man whom I find trying, apart from the battle to
> hang back by the curved ships, for him no longer will there
> by any means to escape the dogs and the vultures.
>
> (*Iliad* II, 391-93)

In fact, the threat of being left to the dogs and ravens became a
conventional part of flyting. Achilles taunts Hector: "the dogs
and the birds will have you all for their feasting",[34] and Odysseus
taunts the fallen Sokos in the same fashion: "the tearing birds
will get you, with their wings close-beating about you. If I die,
the brilliant Achaians will bury me in honor" (*Iliad* XI, 452-55).

Finally, one of the most significant conventions associated
with the hero were his armor and weapons. One has only to
notice the elaborate thirty-line description of the arming of
Agamemnon (*Iliad* XI, 15-46) to appreciate the importance of
the hero's weapons. Even the very appearance of Achilles became
conventional. We are often reminded, in later epics, of the magnificent entrance of Achilles, striking terror into the Trojans:
"But the Trojans, when they heard the brazen voice of Aiakides,/
the heart was shaken in all, and the very floating-maned horses/
turned their chariots about, since their hearts saw the coming
afflictions" (*Iliad* XVIII, 215-17). For one thing, the weapons
and armor symbolize the hero's great stature. No one can wield
the spear of Achilles except him, and when Patroclus dons
Achilles' armor, he must go into battle without the spear. Since
Patroclus is a lesser man, the great armor suffers unaccustomed

---

farers from afar; they lament his loss, and praise his deeds and excellence
as a warrior and leader; the last of their praises was that he had been
among great warriors "most eager for fame". 3137-82.
[34] Iliad XXII, 354. Hector himself uses the same threats against Ajax
(XIII, 829-32) and Patroclus (XVI, 836).

indignities: Phoebus smites Achilles' helmet into the dust and the shield onto the ground – something that had never been permitted to happen to the helmet of the god-like hero. (*Iliad* XVI, 796-99). If Patroclus is not equal to handling the spear, he is not great enough properly to wear the armor; when he disregards Achilles' warning not to follow the Trojans to the walls, and loses the armor to Hector, the discrepancy between the armor and the man is apparent. Even Hector, the greatest of the Trojans and second only to Achilles, is not equal to the honor of wearing Achilles' armor. Zeus warns Hector that he puts on the 'immortal armor of a surpassing man', an honorable symbol which no one but Achilles should wear, and Hector too is doomed when put to the test.

Odysseus too has a weapon which no one else can use – his bow. The bow has a long history (*Odyssey* XXI, pp. 281-82), and Penelope keeps it locked away among the treasures. It serves as a test, separating the false suitors from the true hero; their inability even to string the bow, let alone send an arrow through twelve axes, measures the unheroic character of them all. Odysseus alone has the prowess to string the bow and use the weapon. Beowulf's swords serve the same purpose.[35] Unferth's sword breaks when put to the test, and Beowulf must rely on a supernatural sword which he finds under the mere. Ordinary swords break in his hands.

As a measure of the hero's strength, the armor also indicates his divine origins. The armor Achilles inherits was forged by the gods (XVIII, 83-84), and his new armor, made by Hephaistos, gives him supernatural powers. (*Iliad* XIX, 14). In the *Aeneid*, Vulcan forges Aeneas a sword, corselet of brass, spear, and shield – heaven-sent armor which signifies that the gods sustain him. The delivery of the armor is then signaled by a thunderbolt to foretell that the enemy Laurentines will pay a terrible price (*Aeneid* VIII, 534-38).

Although based on social and political codes sometimes alien to the Christian, these classical conventions, and two important

---

[35] Taylor Culbert, "The Narrative Functions of Beowulf's Swords", *JEGP*, LIX (January, 1960), 13-20.

ones examined in the next chapter – the journey and ceremonial council – were readily adaptable to a new setting, and they sometimes even serve to distinguish between true and false heroic virtue. Of course, certain conventions such as the funeral barrow could not be used except obliquely in a Christian epic, because the Christian identified the elaborate ceremonies with false honor, and denied the value of the burial rites in achieving immortality for the hero. Immortality of a more important kind was achieved in other ways, and it would be blasphemous to accord a Christian hero the funeral rites which honored Achilles. Milton's Christ in both epics has the hereditary traits of the classical epic hero, qualified and modified by a Christian ethic which defines heroic virtue in a very different way. But the very fact that they are used at all should suggest that Christian virtue to these epic poets embraced more than the teaching that a soft answer turneth away wrath. In *The Passion,* Milton speaks of the Christ whom the epic would celebrate as a powerful figure of 'Godlike acts', as well as 'temptations fierce'; [36] this is very much the Christ defined by these conventions as formal epic hero.

The divine origin of epic heroes is, of course, central to Christ. Like Achilles and Aeneas, he is divinely sired, and Satan, in *Paradise Regained,* is acutely aware of it:

> His mother then is mortal, but his Sire,
> Hee who obtains the Monarchy of Heav'n
> And what will he not do to advance his Son?
>
> (I, 86-88)

It is his divine origin – his right to the honors as Son of God – which must be proven in both of Milton's epics. Christ is squarely

---

[36]   He speaks here of feeling constrained by his genre in being unable to celebrate the "labors huge and hard" of his "Most perfect Heroe", as Vida had done in the *Christiad*:

> These latter scenes confine my roving verse,
> To this Horizon is my Phoebus bound;
> His Godlike acts and his temptations fierce,
> And former sufferings other-where are found;
> Loud o'er the rest Cremona's Trump doth sound.

Even at this time, the genre Milton evidently felt most suitable for Christ was the epic.

within the tradition of the young hero of unknown or unproven origin (the incarnation itself embodies the most basic heroic concept – the great figure whom no one recognizes). In *Paradise Lost*, Christ is the untested young hero who must prove that his merit is equal to his great birthright. The reason for Satan's rebellion was an uncertain point among Protestant commentators, who had little to go on for Biblical evidence – a few verses in the Book of Revelation (12: 3-4, 7-9) and a passage in Isaiah (14: 12-15) – and accordingly settled on pride, since it could encompass other possibilities as well,[37] and Milton is no exception (I, 36-40), but he defines the occasion more precisely in epic terms. Satan leads the rebellion in the first place because he will not accept the fact of Christ's birthright – God's command to obey Christ (V, 602-14), the 'just decree' which gives the regal sceptre 'to his only Son by right endu'd' (V, 814-16). In the subsequent action, Christ proves that he is indeed worthy of that sceptre, by his atonement (which thwarts Satan's purposes), and by his victory in the war in heaven. He proves that he "hast been found/ By Merit more than Birthright Son of God" (III, 308-09).

This motif of the young untried hero who must assume his kingdom is one of the principal themes of *Paradise Regained*. Predominant reference to Christ in the poem as the 'Son of God' itself emphasizes his role as the Son. Like Aeneas' kingdom, Christ's has been prophesied (I, 64-65, 70-71), and like Aeneas, he must prove his right to that kingdom. God sends him into the wilderness to meet Satan in order to "show him worthy of his birth divine/ And high prediction" (I, 141-42), and to allow him to prove himself in the world:

> That all the Angels and Ethereal Powers,
> They now, and men hereafter, may discern
> From what consummate virtue I have chose
> This perfect Man, by merit call'd my Son,
> To earn Salvation for the Sons of men.   (I, 163-67)

Christ is the 'obscure, unmarkt, unknown' (I, 24-25) young hero going forth in the world to win his spurs, the young man from

[37]   Patrides, pp. 91-94.

the provinces with nothing to commend him but promise.[38] Mary
has told him that "thou art no son of mortal man .../ Thy Father
is th' Eternal King" (I, 234-36), but men esteem him 'low of
Parentage', and he knows that he must prove himself. His early
life has been 'Private, unactive, calm, contemplative' (II, 81),
and now that he has achieved manhood, he is ready, "I knew the
time/ Now full, that I no more should live obscure,/ But openly
begin" (I, 286-88). Indeed, he is in the same position as his ancestor, the young shepherd David. And his aim, in typically heroic
fashion, is to "learn and know, and thence to do/ What might be
public good".

Obscure and unknown though he is, it is not surprising that
Christ has the aspiring mind. His mother Mary reminds him of
his lineage, "By matchless Deeds express thy matchless Sire" (I,
233), and he is very much aware of the prophecy that he would
'sit on David's throne'. In his youthful obscurity, he aspires to do
great deeds:

> And was admir'd by all: yet this not all
> To which my Spirit aspir'd; victorious deeds
> Flam'd in my Heart, heroic acts; one while
> To rescue *Israel* from the *Roman* yoke,
> Then to subdue and quell o'er all the earth
> Brute violence and proud Tyrannic pow'r,
> Till truth were freed, and equity restor'd   (I, 214-20)

The crux of the matter in *Paradise Regained* is that Christ, like
Aeneas, does not know how he is to attain his kingdom, nor prove
his right to it.[39] His uncertainty about what the messianic fulfill-

---

[38]   Tasso's Rinaldo is also obscure and untested. He was scarcely a man
when he heard the "golden trump ... that soundeth glory, fame, praise in
his ears" (I, 59), and this prompts him to flee "alone, by many an unknown
coast ... till he arrived at the Christian host".

[39]   Christ's heroic role is but one aspect of the pattern; Michael Fixler
(*Milton and the Kingdoms of God* (London, 1964), pp. 221-71) and Barbara
Lewalski ("Theme and Structure in *Paradise Regained*", *SP*, LVII (April,
1960), 186-220) relate the temptations to a three-fold role of prophet, king,
and priest, and to Christ's attempt to understand and realize his mediatorial
role. Compare Merritt Y. Hughes' analysis of Christ's magnanimity as the
ethical focus of the poem (*SP*, XXXV (1938), 254-77) with Arnold Stein's
conclusion that the poem centers upon the four Platonic virtues of wisdom,

ment would mean, and whether it would mean temporal dominion, is also shared by Satan, who has lost his grip on the principle that internal dominion and justice underlie true power. Accordingly, Satan tries to frustrate Christ's kingdom because it means the end of his own 'Reign on Earth so long enjoy'd'; he tempts Christ to prove his divinity, to accept a false conception of his kingdom, to assume his crown before God wills it, or to take the kingdom by the wrong means. Satan spurns Belial's idea to 'set women in his eye' because Christ is formidable enough that he can only be truly tempted by 'Lawful desires of Nature' (II, 230), by "such as have more show/ Of worth, of honor, glory, and popular praise". Christ has nobler ambitions, an aspiring mind, and Satan is shrewd enough to dwell on these:

> And all thy heart is set on high designs,
> High Actions; but wherewith to be achiev'd?
> Great acts require great means of enterprise;
> Thou art unknown, unfriended, low of birth.   (I, 410-13)

Finally, we are reminded by the narrator of Christ's unparalleled success in creating a heroic name. In *Paradise Lost*, like the poet in the *Aeneid* extolling Hercules, Milton adds his own paean to that of the angels in honor of Christ's charity:

> Hail Son of God, Saviour of Men, thy name
> Shall be the copious matter of my Song
> Henceforth, and never shall my Harp thy praise
> Forget, nor from thy Father's praise disjoin.
>   (III, 412-15)

Christ fits the traditional heroic role most completely in quelling the devil legions in *Paradise Lost*.[40] He is reminiscent of the mighty warrior Christ of the Caedmonian Genesis. The battle reaches a stalemate, and Christ steps forth, unsurpassed in strength, assured by God that "the Glory may be thine/ Of ending this great War, since none but Thou/ Can end it" (VI, 701-

---

temperance, justice, and fortitude – all effects of the ultimate cause, heroic knowledge. *Heroic Knowledge*, pp. 17-35.
[40] In *Paradise Lost*, Milton departs from a tradition he accepts in *De Doctrina* (*Works*, XV, 106), that it was Michael who opposed and defeated Satan in the war in heaven. Patrides, pp. 260-61.

03). Milton bestows upon Christ the martial characteristics of the wrathful hero (VI, 824-26). He resembles Achilles and Aeneas going into battle: "into terror chang'd/ His count'nance too severe to be beheld/ And full of wrath bent on his Enemies". Christ's ensign blazes aloft as a sign in heaven (VI, 775-76); Michael's assembled forces retire in silence (VI, 777-84), and Christ, like Achilles, resolves the issue by single combat:

> That they may have thir wish, to try with mee
> In Battle, which the stronger proves, they all,
> Or I alone against them, since by strength
> They measure all. (VI, 818-21)

Christ has an Achillean effect on his enemies: "they astonisht all resistance lost,/ All courage". And he returns in splendid triumph, a mark of glory won:

> With Jubilee advanc'd; and as they went
> Shaded with branching Palm, each order bright,
> Sung Triumph, and him sung Victorious King
> Son, Heir, and Lord, to him Dominion giv'n,
> Worthiest to Reign. (VI, 884-88)

On one hand, heroic virtue in the tradition of Saint Augustine, Saint Thomas, and the Christian epic poets means obedience and charity, reason and self-discipline; on the other, the great Renaissance epics present scenes of great action, martial themes, and heroic deeds. In considering possible contradictions, however, it is necessary to notice Milton's context when he extols patience and suffering. When Adam learns that God accomplishes "great things, by things deem'd weak" (XII, 567), the key word is 'deem'd'. In the fallen world, things 'deem'd' weak are not necessarily weak, but rather mistaken for weakness by the spurious standards of the world, which often mistake the seeming for the real. The passage itself emphasizes the virtue within, and accompanying virtue within is strength without, a principle beyond the grasp of Satan who equates strength with the sword. In this passage, Adam learns the crux of the matter on which all paradoxes are based, "to obey is best/ And love with feare the onely God".

Patience is not a fixed command called for in all circumstances, but rather a response to particular occasions. By the same token, heroic deeds are appropriate only when the occasion requires and when true obedience gives strength and just purpose to the sword in hand. Patience in enduring the evils that befall us "recalls the disturbed and wavering mind to its tranquility; it mitigates, it restores a man to himself".[41] Adam has lost his tranquility by refusing to wait upon the Divine Will, and now must learn patience in accepting the conditions his wilful disobedience has created. The alternative is despair, which underlies Satan's continual defiance of Providence – an exercise in futility that effectively undermines his 'heroism'. Patience and submission to the will of God are prominent in *Paradise Lost*, but not because Milton lost his heroic disposition; Christ's genuine power and heroic style are firmly fixed on a foundation of obedience to God's will, and Adam must be equal to the 'better fortitude/ Of Patience' because he must regain that obedience. Thus the fortitude is 'better' in the sense that once fallen, it is more difficult to regain the inner strength of heroic virtue.

In developing this idea, Tasso, Spenser, and Milton have considerable Scriptural precedent to draw upon. Saint Paul's advice to the Ephesians to "be strong in the Lord, and in the power of his might" (Eph. 6:10) summarizes the traditional connection between strength and obedience, and the metaphor by which he elaborates the idea points to the way in which the connection was symbolized by a militant Christianity:

Put on the whole armour of God, that ye may be able to stand against the wiles of the devil. For we wrestle not against flesh and blood, but against principalities, against powers, against the rule of the darkness of the world, against spiritual wickedness in high places.
Wherefore take unto you the whole armour of God, that ye may be able to withstand in the evil day, and having done all, to stand.
Stand therefore, having your loins girt about with truth, and having on the breastplate of righteousness;
And your feet shod with the preparation of the gospel of peace;
Above all, taking the shield of faith, wherewith ye shall be able to

[41] Lactantius, *The Ante Nicene Christian Library*, eds. Alexander Roberts and James Donaldson (Edinburgh, 1867-72), XXI, 401-02, 347. As quoted in Baumgartner, "Milton and Patience", p. 207.

quench all the fiery darts of the wicked. And take the helmet of
salvation, and the sword of the Spirit, which is the word of God.

(Eph. 6:11-17)

This spiritual field of battle of the Christian calls forth appropriate martial metaphors to express it; against such a formidable enemy, the Christian hero must be armed by God in the
breastplate of righteousness, the shield of faith, and the sword of
the Spirit. With the shield of faith, Spenser's Redcrosse quells the
dragon,[42] and with the sword of the Spirit, Milton's Michael
strikes fear into the hearts of the devils (*P.L.* II, 292-95). The
sword of heroic combat was often used to depict the Word of
God – a two-edged sword that issued from the Lord's mouth
(Rev. 1:16), a symbol of God's power and an instrument of
damnation.[43] When Michael, the martial angel and instrument of
God's justice, meets Satan in single combat, Milton gives his
sword the same significance as did Saint Paul, and Satan's sword,
like that of Turnus facing Aeneas *(Aeneid* XII, 739-41), breaks
in two (VI, 320-27). In short, the sword of the Spirit and the
shield of Faith signify that the Christian is 'strong in the Lord,
and in the power of his might'. In the *Faerie Queene*, Arthur's
great sword, like Michael's, 'flames like a burning brond' (II, iii,
18), and it is irresistible. Tasso's Godfredo gives to Raymond,
one of the few knights whose virtue remains, a special sword
(VII, 72) and a miraculous shield – tokens of unseen divine
support ("And on the shield Argantes' sword was broke" (VII,
92)).

The condition of the hero's weapons and armor are also symbolic of his spiritual condition, his moral progress on the knightly
quest – Guyon's to purge Acrasia's garden, Redcrosse's to
achieve holiness, and Godfredo's to drive the pagans from Jerusalem. The sword and shield of Arthur and Michael are gleaming

[42]   In the letter to Raleigh, Spenser alludes to Saint Paul's words and the
armor which Redcrosse must wear to make his quest a success. Putting on
the armor transforms him from a clownish rustic into "the goodliest man
in al that company". Virgil K. Whitaker, *The Religious Basis of Spenser's
Thought* (Stanford, 1950), pp. 47-48.
[43]   George Wesley Whiting, *Milton and This Pendant World* (Austin,
1959), pp. 47-48.

and bright with use. But Rinaldo's sword reveals how far he has
strayed from his quest. He is the appropriate recipient of the
marvelous sword of the Christian hero, Sweno, but since he has
succumbed to Armida, he is unworthy of the weapon (VIII, 38).
He becomes a false knight, and his weapon hangs in reproach,
symbolic of his forsaken duty. The Christian knights find him
captive in the nets of Armida, his sword, covered with flowers
(XVI, 30). We find Spenser's Cymochles in the same situation,
"In daintie delices and lavish joyes,/ Having his warlike weapons
cast behynd" (II, v, 28); and when Guyon reaches the Bower of
Bliss, he finds, in a fallen young knight, the effects of Acrasia
upon the heroic ideal:

> His warlike armes, the ydle instruments
> Of sleeping praise, were hong upon a tree,
> And his brace shield, full of old moniments,
> Was foully ra'st, that none the signes might see;
> Ne for them, ne for honour, cared hee.   (II, xii, 80)

The rusted shield of this young knight indicates his loss of faith;
the idle weapon, his separation from the Spirit. He has lost the
most important battle – against the powers of darkness and
'spiritual wickedness in high places'. His shield, like those of
Aeneas, Achilles, and Rinaldo, is engraved with scenes of na-
tional greatness, and his ancestors' glory, but it now hangs rusted
and idle, in mockery of his lost faith and forgotten quest.

St. Paul's warning to be 'strong in the Lord' is also expressed
in the Christian hero's contempt for weapons and armor *per se*.
The attitude is seen in Christ who rejects the means of war to gain
his kingdom (*P.R.* III, 400-02), and in Godfredo, who tells the
pagan Aletes that the strength of the Christian forces rests "not
from the trust we have in shield and spear", but in God (II, 85).
Thus Godfredo assaults the pagan fortress with "breastplate fair,
of proof untried,/ Such one as footmen use, light, easy thin", and
leaves behind his "sure and trusty shield, helm and hawberk
strong" (XI, 20-21), because he is sure that God "shall this life
defend, keep, and preserve". And it is perhaps one of the Chris-
tion notes in *Beowulf* that Beowulf spurns his sword and shield
in facing Grendel: "Foe against foe I'll fight to the death,/ And

the one who is taken must trust in God's grace!" (440-41). This paradox has a firm foundation in the epic battle of David and Goliath – certainly one of the best Biblical models for epic heroism we find. David emerges an obscure, untested youth whose strength, though hidden, is immense because it is of the Lord. Goliath, in contrast, is elaborately armed but his strength is only in himself. They combat in typical epic fashion: first mocking one another in a flyting match ("Am I a dog, that thou comest to me with stones?" I Sam. 17:43); then threatening to feed one another to the birds and beasts of the field. Then David explains why he has such confidence against a well-armed giant, and we have a basic principle of Christian heroism:

Thou comest to me with a sword, and with a spear, and with a shield: but I come to thee in the name of the Lord of hosts, the God of the armies of Israel, whom thou hast defied.   (I Sam. 17:45)

In the preceding examples, the dependence and charity of the Christian hero are the direct source of his strength. A correspond-ence of form and spirit is, in fact, a basic quality of moral order to Milton; he characteristically argues in *Colasterion* that when the inner spirit of a marriage is gone, then the form should be dissolved as well.[44] Perhaps the principle is clearest in *Samson Agonistes* – the tragedy of a fallen hero who regains his strength. Samson echoes the confidence of David when confronted by Harapha's brash challenge to do single combat; he accepts against great odds, armed only with his oaken staff:

> Then put on all thy gorgeous arms, thy Helmet
> And Brigandine of brass, thy broad Habergeon,
> Vant-brace and Greaves, and Gauntlet, add thy Spear
> A Weaver's beam, and seven-times folded shield.   (1119-1122)

Harapha suspects some magical arts, but Samson replies that "My trust is in the living God who gave me/ At my Nativity this strength." Since the battle never occurs, it is not certain that Samson's strength is real, in which case his challenge may be rash and premature, even a wish for death, but if his strength is real – symbolized perhaps by his hair growing out – it is the conse-

[44]   *Works* IV, 262.

quence of a faith regained in God. Like the apple in Eden, the secret of Samson's hair symbolizes his continual obedience – the test on which hinges his strength. Giving away his secret in disobedience of God's command, he has isolated himself from the source of his power, and finds himself in chains, a prisoner of the enemy Philistines, alone, and blind. His regeneration is also an inward change reflected by the return of his powers. If a thorough correspondence of form and spirit, of martial strength and inner virtue, is essential to Christian heroic virtue, then the sword and shield may symbolize equally well the strength of humble obedience, or the weakness and dishonor of vainglorious ambition.

Correspondence as a feature of heroism is practically universal. The figure of the proven hero whose magnificence and impressive appearance match his accomplishments admits of several variations which themselves emphasize the principle. Considerable suspense and interest are afforded by the unproven hero who emerges, like the shepherd David, in a low and humble appearance, to astound the mighty. A variation on this theme is the proven hero who, like Odysseus, suffers temporary misfortunes which cause him to be found in an appearance unworthy of his nature: in a low disguise, he is able to determine who is corrupt in his home. The action then centers upon the hero's return, and exploits some of the same possibilities as are found in the young hero emerging. The false hero, or villain, often gains honors and trust because people customarily take the form for the spirit, in which case the action may include a climactic unmasking. The villain is of a different species, however, from the fool who, like Braggadocchio, turns the process around and thinks that by acquiring the forms of heroism, he will thereby acquire the spirit, the strength and skill which come only from within.

Both Tasso and Spenser show considerable interest in the relation of form and spirit. Arthur's high quest and inner virtue are reflected in his magnificent appearance, in 'glitterand armour', in a "haughtie helmet, horrid all with gold,/ Both glorious brightnesse and great terrour bredd". Spenser takes seven stanzas merely to describe him (*F.Q.* I, vii, 29-36). The gold on his helmet glitters like the gold in Milton's heaven. The principle is seen in reverse in his portrayal of the ruined carcasses of high nobles who committed themselves to the house of pride, soon resembling outwardly their inner corruption (I, v, 49-53). The order of events in Book I of the *Faerie Queene* illuminates the relation between inward virtue and heroic action: the entire book prepares Redcrosse for killing the dragon. He slowly changes from a clownish rustic into a knight as he gains in virtue, and is not properly equipped to kill the dragon until he has entered the House of Holiness and learned wisdom atop the Hill of Contemplation. In *Jerusalem Delivered*, the defeat of the pagans follows upon the death of Armida. The Christians are weakened and threatened with defeat when Godfredo's ten knights stray from the quest: Rinaldo's loss to the Christians follows directly upon the disorder which results when Armida's temptations succeed, and his return symbolizes the return of virtue. Tasso himself equates the siege of Jerusalem with the Holy War in man, and the Christian army with the individual soul under the rule of Reason.[45] God sends Michael's heavenly legions to help the Christians overrun the city (XVIII, 92) only after Rinaldo has resisted Armida and returned to Godfredo. The action symbolizes the superior strength which accompanies true obedience and charity.

This principle of correspondence – the crux of Christ's heroic virtue – makes it imperative to view his dependence on God and martial splendor not as contradictory but as complementary. That his martial splendor should reflect his obedience and charity is no more difficult to understand than the parallel idea that true freedom consists only in obedience and self-discipline. Christ exemplifies Abdiel's assertion that "he who in debate of Truth hath Won,/ Should win in Arms, in both disputes alike/ Victor" (VI, 122-24). Christ's definition of true kingship in *Paradise Regained* well illustrates the principle. The man who would be king must first rule himself, for whoever is "Subject himself to Anarchy within,/ Or lawless passions in him, which he serves" (*P.R.* II, 471-72) can never rule a nation wisely. Furthermore, the true ruler rules not only himself, but also the 'nobler part' of the body

45   Fairfax, p. 438.

politic: his wise rule over the body (the exercise of power symbolized by the sceptre) is the consequence of his wise rule over
the soul, the 'inner part' of the nation:

> ... to guide Nations in the way of truth
> By saving Doctrine, and from error lead
> To know, and knowing worship God aright,
> Is yet more Kingly.   (II, 473-75)

The earthly kingdom must be guided as a part of God's kingdom,
and Christ affirms that when the sceptre is used for this purpose,
it is a worthy thing indeed. By the same token, when the sceptre
is misused, one must look within for reasons. Satan shows Christ
the grandeur of Rome (IV, 45-60), a place similar to Pandemonium, and Christ points out that it is a sham, that in fact the
outward yoke the Romans bear is a tangible manifestation of
their inner spirit, 'by themselves enslav'd'. Since Rome cannot
govern herself, she governs badly her subject nations.

Satan offers Christ the sceptre, the sword, and the lamp as
things worthy in themselves and as a means to gain wealth, power
or glory, but Christ replies that they are worthy only if they
answer to the Spirit. To Christ, riches "are needless ... both for
themselves/ and ... To Gain a Sceptre", and the same is true
of wealth offered to win an empire, or an empire to win glory
(III, 44-46). Christ does not, however, reject the sceptre because
it is a sceptre, or in a spirit of renunciation. In *Paradise Lost*, the
sceptre is a symbol of his duty, given to him by God and taken
away when he has accomplished it. God foresees that Christ's
rule over a fallen world will extend until the Judgment Day, at
which time he will lay down the sceptre (III, 339-41). Christ
accepts the sceptre in a spirit of true obedience and uses it only
as a means to a higher end. In fact, Christ labels Stoic virtue as
'Philosophic pride' (*P.R.* IV, 300-08), and Milton elsewhere rejects 'Stoical apathy' as 'inconsistent with true patience'.[46] Heroic
virtue in Milton is gained through no simple alternatives: neither
seeking nor avoiding will serve as general principles, for each

---

[46] *Christian Doctrine* II, x. *Works* XVII, 253. Hughes, *Complete Poems*,
p. 522n.

occasion demands a separate choice.[47] Whether acting or refraining, accepting or rejecting, the 'just man' whom God would mark with approbation must preserve a difficult balance, guided by his reason and 'by his own dignity rightly understood':

The virtues more peculiarly appropriate to a high station are lowliness of mind and magnanimity. Lowliness of mind consists in thinking humbly of ourselves, and in abstaining from self-commendation, except where occasion requires it. . . .[48] Magnanimity is shown, when in seeking or avoiding, the acceptance of refusal of riches, advantages, or honors, we are actuated by a regard to our own dignity rightly understood.[49]

The point at issue is clearly not the riches or honors themselves, as Milton goes on to illustrate:

Thus Abraham did not refuse the gifts of the king of Egypt, Gen. xii.13.x.14 though he rejected those of the king of Sodom, xiv.22,23. and though he declined to accept the field offered him by Ephron the Hittite, except on payment of its full value, xxiii.13 Thus also Job, although restored to his former health and prosperity, did not disdain the congratulatory offering of his friends, xlii.11. In this spirit Gideon refused the kingdom, Judges viii.23. . . . Such was also the spirit of Nehemiah in asking honors, ii.5. . . . of Samuel in laying down his authority, I. Sam. x.1. . . . of Christ in rejecting the empire of the world, Matt. iv.9. . . . in despising riches, 2 Cor. viii.9. . . . in accepting honors, Matt. xxi.7. . . . Such finally is the spirit by which every Christian is guided in his estimate of himself.[50]

When Satan argues that God requires glory from men, Christ does not reply in the negative, but adds "And reason". When God commands temperance, only the Satanic temper construes it as abstinence or renunciation, for what Christ renounces, he must renounce for good reasons. It is difficult for him to refrain from

[47] Arnold Stein concludes that the ascetic potentialities of such a prolonged temptation are carefully contained: "There is no rejecting of the natural world in hate. What is rejected is the perverted natural world, or the natural world threatening to pervert – to pervert true order and the true basis of man's possible joy in the free exercise of his functions." *Heroic Knowledge*, p. 35.

[48] Milton quotes Job to illustrate the proper occasion: "I have understanding as well as you, I am not inferior to you (Job xii:3); what ye know, do I know also" (Job 13:2). *Works* XVII, 237.

[49] *Works* XVII, 235-41.

[50] *Works* XVII, 241-43.

acting in *Paradise Regained* because, as we have seen, his nature inclines towards deeds. In such a context, refraining is neither negative nor easy. Nor does *Paradise Regained* present the active and contemplative ideals as opposing alternatives. To be sure, Satan turns from one to the other when it seems that Christ "seem'st otherwise inclin'd/ Than to a worldly Crown, addicted more/ To contemplation and profound dispute". But he finds to his exasperation that Christ applies the same rigorous standard to contemplative ideals:

> Since neither wealth, nor honor, arms nor arts,
> Kingdom nor Empire pleases thee, nor aught
> By me propos'd in life contemplative,
> Or active, tended on by glory, or fame,
> What dost thou in this world?   (*P.R.* IV, 368-72)

Many readers have felt that Satan's question is entirely just, but this misses the point. Even in hell, the devils make no choice between heroic deeds and heroic endurance (*P.L.* I, 157-58, II, 199-200); realizing that the proposals of neither Moloch nor Belial would raise their fallen lot, they proceed to a more devilish plan. Christ does not give up an unworthy world in order to gain the next, but rather rejects both active and contemplative ideals of the world because, as Satan offers them, they can only be misused, in conflict with the moral hierarchy of God.

Thus Milton does not replace the Homeric ideal with a nobler heroism of 'patient suffering', but with much the same emphasis on the heroic test of discipline and temperance that we find in Tasso and Spenser. Michael shows Adam warfare and violence based on the false standards of the fallen world (*P.L.* XI, 689-99), and Adam learns that it will be necessary for him to suffer for truth's sake in finding the way back, but nowhere does Milton feel the need to justify the true deeds of martial valor which Christ performs in the war in heaven, or the heroic aspirations of the young hero of *Paradise Regained*. When Adam asks how Christ is to bruise the serpent's heel, and Michael replies "Dream not of thir fight/ As of a duel", it is gratuitous to read this as a rejection of martial valor, for the real issue is the inner spirit of obedience and love necessary to withstand the temptations of the ever-present antagonist, "Not by destroying *Satan*, but his works/ In thee and in thy Seed" (VII, 394-95). In this light, it is reasonable to suggest that Milton's skeptical reference to the tinsel trappings of knighthood (IX, 25-41) is actually a comparison between a romance knighthood of empty trappings ('fabl'd Knights/ In Battles feign'd') and an epic knighthood in which obedience and charity give substance to those trappings. The imagery of the passage emphasizes the externals which themselves have nothing to do with heroism, but rather parody it when the inner spirit of obedience is missing. Milton's reference to a 'higher argument' puts the focus where it belongs and where it is dramatized in Book IX – within the character of the hero. In this sense, Adam's temptation is a higher argument, and 'more Heroic' than the wrath of Achilles because it focuses on the inner test. It is not Achilles' battlefield prowess that falls short of true heroic virtue but rather his self-centered pursuit of Honor – in Milton's view, a motive which would undermine prowess.

The fortitude of patience is often rather the lot of the fallen hero. Blind Samson is in much the same situation as fallen Adam: in fact, the Chorus weighs the alternatives of active deeds and patience, and advises him exactly what Michael counsels Adam:

> Oh how comely it is and how reviving
> To the Spirits of just men long opprest!
> When God into the hands of thir deliverer
> Puts invincible might
> To quell the mighty of the Earth, th' oppressour. . . .
> But patience is more oft the exercise
> Of Saints, the trial of thir fortitude,
> Making them each his own Deliverer,
> And Victor over all
> That tyrannie or fortune can inflict,
> Either of these is in thy lot,
> *Samson*, with might endu'd
> Above the Sons of men; but sight bereav'd
> May chance to number thee with those
> Whom Patience finally must crown (1268-1296)

It may be noted here that patience is not elevated as a higher or more heroic alternative. The point is that Samson's blindness precludes the first ("but sight bereav'd/ May chance to number

thee ... with those/ Whom Patience finally must crown"), and
when we recall that the blindness is also his spiritual blindness in
disobeying God, it is evident that his struggle at this point is with
despair. Both magnanimity and patience are manifestations of
fortitude, but patience is not the greater, though it may be the
more difficult. Milton is saying here that patient fortitude is
'more oft' the option of man because heroic magnanimity is so
rare. Samson is one of God's rare champions, but his failure to
obey empties him of strength, and he then must exhibit a different
sort of fortitude – faith in God's mercy which overcomes despair.
The Christian model of heroic virtue must suffer or do as the
occasion requires, but he is the only one who has a choice of a
time to do or a time to suffer. Having fallen, he can only suffer.

   Moreover, the spirit which impels the patient suffering makes
all the difference. Patience is not an end in itself, for false patience
or misguided humility are as helpless in overcoming adversity as
false valor is. It must be remembered that patience is the advice
of Belial no less than it is of Michael. With 'words cloth'd in
reason's garb', Belial advises 'ignoble ease and peaceful sloth',
but in the same terms that Michael uses in advising Adam. He
argues that to combat God is futile, hence their best alternative
is to endure patiently their fate, a fortitude that they are able to
exhibit as well as the fortitude of heroic deeds ("To suffer, as to
do,/ Our strength is equal"). Belial counsels patience, not the
patience that requires a faith in God and hope in his mercy, but
the patience of despair, based on the premise of God's indiffer-
ence and further alienation; he assumes that God will remit the
pain and punishment because in time he will no longer care:

> . . . which if we can sustain and bear,
> Our Supreme Foe in time may much remit
> His anger, and perhaps thus far remov'd
> Not mind us not offending, satisfi'd
> With what is punish't; whence these raging fires
> Will slack'n, if his breath stir not thir flames.
>
> (II, 209-14)

Belial's patience proceeds from a willingness to remain in their
present alienation, having lost the good not missing it, "since our

present lot appears/ For happy though but ill, for ill not worst,/ If we procure not to ourselves more woe" (II, 222-25). It is a gross parody of the patience and fortitude that Michael defines for Adam.

Central to Milton's sense of heroic virtue is an exact correspondence of form and spirit such as that expressed in Spenser's couplet, "For of the soule the bodie forme doth take,/ For soule is forme, and doth the bodie make." Christ's inner virtues of obedience and charity give strength, substance, and direction to his public virtues – the sceptre of kingship, and the sword of martial valor. At all times, his martial splendor, his ambition, and Achillean wrath reflect accurately his dependence as the servant as well as the Son of God. He is neither a passive figure renouncing the world, nor a puzzling, scornful knight, but a hero whose outward acts and choices, whatever they may involve, always mirror obedience and charity within. Milton rejects the heroic motives of Achilles and all other forms of violence done for the wrong ends, but he does not reject the sword itself, or the active deeds which the Christian hero may need to perform, as, at other times, he must exercise a temperate renunciation, in the service of the Lord. The Christian way of walking in the way of the Lord, defined for Adam by the heroic pattern of Christ, does not invariably lead to patient suffering, for endurance is not a higher alternative to Homeric deeds but a necessary part of a broader definition of heroic virtue which may encompass both. Christ renounces the worldly realms offered by Satan, offers to sacrifice himself for the race of man, and dons the armor of God to wage war: for kingly rule, knowledge, and martial power are but spokes of a wheel whose hub is true obedience, and no one of these is necessarily in conflict with the others, or with patience. Perhaps an appropriate summary of the heroic virtue of Milton's Christ, as well as an introduction to the character of Satan, is found in the definition of true knighthood of a twelfth-century preacher, Alanus de Insulis:

For external knighthood is a figure for internal knighthood, and without the internal, the external is vain and empty. And just as there are two parts of a man, corporal and spiritual, so there are two swords

proper to defense against various enemies of man; the material, with
which injuries are repelled, and the spiritual, with which those things
which injure the mind are repelled. Whence it is said, 'Behold, here
are two swords' (Luke 22:38). The knight should gird on the external
one to keep temporal peace from violence, and the internal one,
which is the sword of the Word of God, to restore peace to his own
breast.[51]

[51]   *De arte praedicatoria*, PL, 210, col. 186. Quoted in D. W. Robertson, Jr., *A Preface to Chaucer: Studies in Medieval Perspective* (Princeton,
1962), pp. 174-75.

II

SATAN THE ANTI-HERO

If Milton's 'fit audience' have left Christ largely to himself to practice that quiet, contemplative wisdom attributed to him, they have by contrast accorded Satan the notoriety and attention of a worldly hero. In this respect, Nature has imitated Art. He has been given greater attention because he is by nature more elusive, as it were, rarely observed except darkly through a glass. In the normal order of things, in the pristine perfection of prelapsarian Eden and the state of true virtue, there is a precise correspondence of form and spirit. But with the advent of evil in the world – the fall of Satan and the subsequent fall of Adam – correspondence was disrupted with immense and far-reaching complications. Saint Thomas says that evil always exists joined with a good,[1] and Richard Hooker gives much the same idea: "For evil as evil cannot be desired: if that be desired which is evil, the cause is the goodness which is or seemeth to be joined with it." [2] It is thus difficult to perceive evil in a world where good and evil are joined and appearances do not necessarily reflect realities.

The dilemma which this fact poses for Right Reason is a

[1] Since evil has no being or nature of its own (by definition, the being and perfection of any nature is good), it must exist in conjunction with a good. He cites Dionysius (Div. Nom. IV): "Evil does not act, nor is it desired, except by virtue of some good joined to it." *Summa Theologica*, I, Ia, Q. 48, Art. I.
[2] *Laws of Ecclesiastical Polity*, I, vii, 6. *The Works of Richard Hooker*, ed. John Keble (London, 1888), I, 233. Hooker says "there is no particular object so good, but it may have the shew of some difficulty or unpleasant quality annexed to it, in respect whereof the Will may shrink and decline it; contrariwise (for so things are blended) there is no particular evil, which hath not some appearance of goodness whereby to insinuate itself."

major theme in Renaissance literature, where villainy customarily prospers by quoting Scripture. Spenser's Archimago masquerades at one time as a Christian knight (so convincingly that "Saint George himselfe ye would have deemed him to be"; *F.Q.* I, ii, 11), at another, as a holy man of heavenly contemplation. Shakespeare ironically emphasizes the 'honesty' of Iago, and in *Measure for Measure* Angelo boldly warns Isabella that his unsoiled name, the austerity of his former life, and his high place in the state protect him: "Say what you can, my false o'erweighs your true" (II, iv). Malcolm realizes how difficult it is to distinguish the true from the false when they appear the same:

> Angels are bright still, though the brightest fell.
> Though all things foul would wear the brows of grace,
> Yet grace must still look so.   (*Macbeth* IV, iii)

And Milton says that the "knowledge of good is so involv'd and interwoven with the knowledge of evill, and in so many cunning resemblances hardly to be discern'd, that those confused seeds which were impos'd on *Psyche* as an incessant labour to cull, and sort asunder, were not more intermixt." [3] He attributes part of the difficulty to man's psychology, and in so doing, gives an apt description of many a wayward response to Satan:

For Truth, I know not how, hath this unhappiness fatal to her, ere she can come to the trial and inspection of the understanding; being to pass through many little wards and limits of the several affections and desires, she cannot shift it, but must put on such colors and attire as those pathetic handmaids of the soul please to lead her in to their queen ... And contrary, when any falsehood comes that way, if they like the errand she brings, they are so artful to counterfeit the *very shape and visage* of Truth, that the understanding ... sentences for the most part one for the other at the first blush. [4]

The poor 'understanding' has not improved its position since. If Satan was naturally elusive to the seventeenth century, the passing of time has buried the concepts according to which he was conceived, and the modern reader – approaching him in the wake of a tradition romantically fascinated with the powers of

---

[3]   *Works*, IV, 310-11.
[4]   *Works*, III, 249.

darkness and rebellion, and more recently preoccupied with the inner drama of the mind – has a variety of Satans to choose from.[5] From Blake's supposition that Milton was of the devil's party in his creation of Satan, Shelley could admire Milton as a fellow revolutionary, and the Reverend Samuel Roberts (*Milton Unmasked*, 1844) could call *Paradise Lost* 'one of the most unholy, uninteresting, and mischievous books that was ever published'. The twentieth century perpetuates the impression with more sophistication: Milton's fascination with Satan has been relegated to the subconscious [6] and made a point of departure for criticism of artistic problems.[7]

[5] Werblowsky sees a heroic Prometheus, *Lucifer and Prometheus;* C. S. Lewis catches a glimpse of Braggadocchio, *A Preface to Paradise Lost,* pp. 93ff.; Empson envisages a kind of peasant leader in futile revolt against a tyrannous Czar, *Milton's God* (London, 1961), p. 146; John Crowe Ransom interpreted Satan as a Promethean symbol of the scientific enlightenment, *God Without Thunder* (London, 1931), pp. 131-40.

[6] Assuming that Milton's art expressed his innermost feelings, Denis Saurat identified Milton with Satan and argued that Milton was most himself when his verse reflects passion: "The deep pleasure he takes in his creation of Satan is the joy of liberating, purging himself of the evil in himself, by concentrating it, outside himself, into a work of art." *Milton: Man and Thinker* (New York, 1925), p. 220; E. M. W. Tillyard suggested the same thing in *Milton* (London, 1930), pp. 277-78, but changed his mind in *The Miltonic Setting* (New York, 1951), pp. 53-61, with the view that Milton's sympathy for Satan is no more than a reflection of the Satan in all of us. J. B. Broadbent takes a more esoteric interest, speculating on what seem to be pecularities in Milton's good and evil characters, for example, his finding that Milton hates Belial too much: "It was probably fear of his own voluptuousness, and perhaps of a homosexual tendency caused by his too-devoted father, with mixed pride and shame in his own physical beauty and his role as a man of letters rather than action, that impelled him to fondle every manifestation of Belialism, and then crush it with masculine hard rationality." *Some Graver Subject* (London, 1960), p. 93. Werblowsky assumes that something undermines the poem and searches for reasons in Jungian psychology. By a process of telescoping incidental similarities between Satan and Prometheus into a full-fledged identification, he is able to conclude that the strange dynamism and attraction of Satan are really archetypal murmurings of the human soul expressing themselves through the soul of Milton. F. R. Leavis sees Milton where Milton intended Satan and concludes that Satan is inconsistently conceived because Milton's "own substance" got the upper hand. *The Common Pursuit* (London, 1952), pp. 20-28.

[7] Analyzing two Satans which he sees emerging inconsistently, A. J. A. Waldock concludes that Milton changed his mind (or suddenly became

Probably the most defensible and prevailing view of Satan is that Milton consciously made him magnificent in the pattern of Achilles so as to discredit the old Homeric heroism by exposing its shortcomings to the Miltonic ideal of patient suffering.[8] The effect of such a contrast is ironically the reverse of its intention, which is to stress the spirit within, for both patience and valor are external manifestations, and when they are made the point at issue, the essence of heroic virtue is obscured. If patient endurance is greater than battlefield valor, then the Homeric features of Christ and Abdiel crop up as oddities bestowed on Milton by his genre, like a rusty suit of armor inherited from a disreputable relative. To a degree the Homeric features of Satan serve as static characterization, defining anti-heroic dimensions of the Satanic nature, for example, his self-centered pursuit of Honor; but in a more important respect, these forms define a transfor-

---

aware of what he had created), then indulged in a technique of degradation, a mechanical and unconvincing process of stripping away Satan's heroic magnificence. In effect presupposing that Milton was unconsciously a Satanist, consciously a Christian, Waldock theorizes that Milton was carried away with admiration for Satan, then became "nervous" at what he had created, and, since he could not change him (because what he had written was part of an "organic whole"), he began to degrade him with unsatisfactory results. *Paradise Lost and Its Critics*, pp. 81-82; Closely following Waldock in restricting his vision to what is "actually in the poem", John Peter takes Satan's deterioration for a coarsening of technique which allows our interest in Satan to drain away. Our interest naturally gravitates away from Satan and toward Adam and Eve when they appear, by what Peter calls a "polarization of human contact" principle. In charting Satan's course, he finds a "bumpy and uncertain curve": Satan is up (Books I-II), then down (Book IV), then up again (Book VI). *A Critique of Paradise Lost*, pp. 50-62. Such a criticism is untenable because Peter seemingly ignores the convention of beginning *in medias res*, and observes only the narrative, not the real chronology. Since the beginning of the story is Satan's rebellion in heaven, the archangel of Book VI should certainly be more magnificent than the fallen Satan of Book IV, and instead of a structural weakness, we have further evidence of a coherent and consistent decline.

[8]   See C. M. Bowra, *From Virgil to Milton*, pp. 227-29; Maurice McNamee, *Honor and the Epic Hero*, pp. 174-75; Davis P. Harding, *The Club of Hercules: Studies in the Classical Background of Paradise Lost* (Urbana, 1962); Douglas Bush, "The Isolation of the Renaissance Hero", in *Reason and the Imagination*, ed. Joseph Mazzeo (New York, 1962), pp. 57-69.

mation in that nature made evident by his increasing inability even to match the standard of Achilles. Satan descends the scale of being to the point that, in a manner of speaking, he is no more able to handle the bow of Odysseus than are Penelope's suitors, or wield the spear of Achilles. Satan is a mighty and condemned figure in gradual eclipse, and the old heroic conventions define the change that overtakes him, from Books V-VI to Books I-II, and finally IX-X. A grandeur and nobility that is fundamentally malign finally loses even its appearance.

Satan is not modeled upon any single epic figure: parallels occur within the context of three larger conventions – the battlefield, the council, and the journey. When Satan is on his journey, Milton emphasizes certain parallels with Odysseus and Aeneas; when in the council, Satan resembles Agamemnon; when on the battlefield, Turnus and Hector.[9] His basic role is that of Hector and Turnus – an antagonist who fails in the final encounter with the hero because he falls short of the heroic standard. But Satan is as different from Turnus as Turnus is from Hector, even though they use the same conventions, because Milton's standard of heroism is new. In fact, Satan's essential position fits neither the old hero nor the old antagonist. Homeric conventions and parallels to the old heroism are useful to Milton in presenting Satan's false heroism, but they are not the thing itself, because Satan is defined against the standard of heroism seen in Christ. In fact, Satan cannot be wholly understood except in relation to Christ. The two of them together give us an understanding of the real contrast between them, and the reasons for the apparent similarities in many details of characterization. Together they represent antithetical moral attitudes which are, to Adam, alternative patterns of conduct; at one point, Adam follows in the tradition of heroes who fall; at another, he abandons Satan's way and discovers the meaning for him of the pattern of heroism in

[9] John Steadman suggests a three-fold Satanic ancestry useful to consider: the Achilles type (Ajax, Turnus, Rinaldo); the Odysseus type; and the leader who must preserve order and discipline among his legions (Agamennon, Aeneas, Godfredo). "Image and Idol: Satan and the Element of Illusion in *Paradise Lost*", *JEGP*, LIX (October, 1960), p. 648.

Christ. A brief look at Satan's lineage as battlefield antagonist will show how the concept of the antagonist changed, and also what kind of antagonist Milton creates from old materials.

Hector, the antagonist of heroic Achilles, has been admired through the ages as one of the noblest figures in literature. He is the prototype of great antagonists: whenever the hero must cope with a real antagonist, and not a corrupt system (such as Robin Hood and Cyrano face), the antagonist is made of the same stuff as the hero, whether it be a nobility that is misplaced in a losing cause or a great stature inverted and malign. In fact Hector is admired partly because he is the antagonist champion of a losing cause: the ages have sympathized with him because noble though he is, he is fated to lose. That Achilles should have such an enemy gives a strong pathos to events. These two champions, cut from the same pattern and united by a common nobility and honor, engage in a conflict unworthy of them; this makes Hector's inevitable defeat seem that much more a tragic and pointless ruin. There is nothing false about Hector, but rather a flaw characteristic of the hero of tragedy. He ignores Polydamus' warning to stay within the walls and must face Achilles realizing that what has sealed his fate and endangered Troy is his own *hybris*:

Now, since by my own recklessness I have ruined my people, I feel shame before the Trojans and the Trojan women with trailing robes, that someone who is less of a man than I will say of me: "Hektor believed in his own strength and ruined his people."

(*Iliad* XXII, 104-07)

If Virgil's hero, Aeneas, is much different from Achilles, so his antagonist, Turnus, is much different from Hector. The tragic possibilities of great-souled Hector are not realized in Turnus; he is more of a Roman Achilles (the ancestor of Hotspur and Laertes), self-centered, headstrong and valiant but not reflective or possessed of a responsible conscience. Turnus does not have the depth of character and the sense of duty of Hector, nor does he arouse the same sympathy as the loser. He is not, like Hector, a husband and father with a home to lose and an inner conflict of love and honor, but a single warrior, like Achilles, whose bride is a symbol to him of his battlefield honors. He does not exhibit

Hector's tragic awareness of his fate, nor does his doom signal a general doom. Latinus' kingdom is not doomed by Turnus' death but promised a new start toward something greater. In effect, Virgil models the antagonist's role on the character of Achilles. In the many parallels between Turnus and Achilles (Turnus is called a 'second Achilles', VI, 89), one finds that the virtues of Achilles have now become limitations in Turnus, judged as he is by the higher standard of heroism in Aeneas. Turnus is enraged at losing the daughter of King Latinus to Aeneas; like Achilles, he has been cheated of an honor earned in battle, and he has a strong sense of injured merit (VII, 421-24). In Book IX, he emerges on the field like Achilles, "the blood-red plumes flicker on his head, and lightnings shoot sparkling from his shield" (IX, 731-32); and he tells Pandarus "here too shalt thou tell that a Priam found his Achilles" (IX, 741). But this wrath is now a distinct limitation, the rage of a warrior unable to control himself; it spoils the plan of attack and prevents his victory:

... had the conqueror forthwith taken thought to burst the bars and let in his comrades at the gate, that had been the last day of the war and of the nation. But rage and mad thirst of slaughter drive him like fire on the foe.[10]   (IX, 756-60)

There is a parallel, incidentally, between the roles of Patroclus and Pallas, the young comrades of Achilles and Aeneas. Both are lesser men, killed when they venture to fight the antagonist while the hero is away. Their deaths then give Achilles and Aeneas special cause for revenge, in effect, impelling the hero's return and the resolution of the conflict. Hector kills Patroclus, and wears the fatal armor into combat against Achilles: Turnus kills Pallas and wears the fatal sword-belt into battle against Aeneas. Milton is not explicit about these conventions, but there is a similarity to the situation of Satan, Adam, and the Son, 'one greater Man', who undoes what the antagonist has done to Adam.

[10]   Much like Turnus is Juno, his godly sponsor, who has his exaggerated sense of honor, his anger, and his lust for violence. Still smarting from the Trojan war and the judgment of Paris, Juno stirs up the winds to shipwreck Aeneas (I, 34-123), and inflames the Rutulians against him because she wants to protect Carthage.

The hero of *Paradise Lost* defeats Satan after Satan has brought death to Adam.

These conventions associated with the classical antagonist – his vulnerability because forsaken by the gods, his early triumph over the lesser hero, his defense of a doomed kingdom, and the rashness or *hybris* which brings about his fall – were easily modi-fied to the Christian epic, and all of them define Satan. The con-ventions of character and situation thus pass from epic to epic, but a new kind of conflict emerges. Only a difference in degree separates Hector from Achilles, and to a lesser extent, this is true of Aeneas and Turnus. Turnus exhibits the self-centered old values, but he is also heroic and noble. In the Christian subject, on the other hand, the battle of hero and antagonist is a conflict of good and evil, and the antagonist is much more a villain than ever he was in Homer and Virgil. Satan is originally of the angels and has the stature of the evil powers in high places that Saint Paul recognized, but the changes that take place because of the fall finally make him different not in degree but in kind. The contrast between the Son of God and Satan is no conflict of equals; Satan's fall is a fall on the scale of being, and he becomes not a heroic antagonist but an anti-hero. Moreover, the rules of warfare are now different: no bond of honor cuts across the con-flict for the hero to share with the antagonist. Satan's *hybris* is nothing less than pride and presumption, and he dooms himself and his 'people' by rejecting God and the strength that accom-panies obedience. At bottom, the substance of Satan is virtually a direct inversion of the obedience and charity of Christ – pride and malice.[11] In general, Satan manifests pride toward God and malice toward Adam, and displays these vices in the larger con-

---

[11] Of course, the contrast has a greater range than is signified by these terms and is perhaps better suggested by the contrasts of Virtue and Vice which Milton lists in *Christian Doctrine*. Dependence includes the special virtues of duty towards God: Love, Trust, Hope, Gratitude, Fear, Humility, Patience, and Obedience. Their corresponding vices, under the heading of Pride, are: hatred, distrust, presumption, doubt, despair, ingratitude, slavish fears, false humility, impatience under the divine decrees, and disobedience (*Works* XVII, 51-71). Charity, the virtues of one's duty towards man, in-cludes humanity, good will, compassion and brotherly love; and the corre-sponding vices – encompassed by malice – include hatred, envy, unmer-

ventions of battlefield, council, and journey. The structure of the infernal council illustrates Satan's pride and presumption; the motive of his quest, his malice: conversely, the heavenly council exhibits Christ's obedience; the great quest he undertakes for man, his charity. In these conventions emerges a clear polarity of hero and anti-hero.

Evil traditionally appears in the guise of goodness, however, and falsehood resembles the truth. As a result, the difference is not always obvious, and we are often rather appalled at the similarities than comforted by the contrasts. The hero resembles the anti-hero because the problem of good and evil is inherently epistemological. The Christian tradition faced the timeless human problem of distinguishing truth from illusion, of reconciling a presupposed ideal order with an imperfect imitation of it in the natural world, by pointing to the fall. In Adam's fall, as hell and chaos encroached on earth, good became mingled with evil, and the quest for virtue became inseparably a search for truth. Adam fell from truth as well as from innocence, and with the mingling of good and evil, man's existence became a continual struggle even to perceive the difference. Man's only guide through this dark wood – the only means by which he can separate the good from evil elements and reconstruct the virtue and perfection he has lost – is his Right Reason, and since the fall, even this is lamentably fallible.[12] When a vision appears to a Christian, he has no easy way of knowing whether it comes from God or the devil. It is this murky state of affairs which is represented in Satan's resemblance to Christ. It presents to man a subtle illusion despite the fact that the divine order of God prevails with respect to Satan himself.[13] As an archangel, Satan originally has a heroic

---

cifulness, hypocritical charity, preposterous love, and rivalry (*Works* XVII, 257-67).

[12] Saint Thomas was more optimistic about the matter, but Saint Augustine's stress on the corruptive effects of original sin on man's will, and man's consequent dependence on God for finding his way in the darkness, was more influential during the Reformation. See Patrides, *Milton and the Christian Tradition*, pp. 97-108.

[13] For the distinction between God's positive Will, which created good, and God's permissive Will, which allowed evil and yet in no way reduces

appearance; but the narrative follows his unsuccessful attempts to sustain an impressive martial appearance which the spirit within will no longer support, and in his gradual decline from archangel to metamorphosed serpent, a new correspondence occurs.

As we observed, Milton does not equate the sword and shield with false heroism: Christ appears in martial array. Hence when Satan appears in the same garb, it is misleading to suppose that Milton is rejecting Homeric standards by giving Satan the role. The old standard of Achilles does not represent a sufficient departure from Christian virtue to define adequately the false heroism in the Christian antagonist. His scorn for booty, for example, is hardly a Satanic feature, and in some ways Achilles is a most compelling figure. Achilles' wrath becomes in Turnus an ungovernable rage, and it also appears in the false knights of Spenser and Tasso: Spenser's intemperate Pyrochles is easily subdued by Guyon because his rage renders him awkward in battle (*F.Q.* II, v, 8-11); likewise, in *Jerusalem Delivered*, the epitome of Achillean wrath is pagan Argantes, so angry battling Tancred that he becomes confused: "Desire of vengeance so o'ercame his senses,/ That he forgot all dangers, all defenses" (VI, 45-46). But wrath is no more essential to false heroism than are pride in military prowess, a sense of injured merit, or the guile which the Renaissance saw in Ulysses. Like the symbolism of darkness and isolation, they are manifestations of Satan's false heroism, but the essence is something else, and it is a distortion of Achilles and Turnus to equate them with Satan, for the contexts are very different.[14] If the substance of true heroism is obedience and charity, the false shadow is Satan's malice and pride. Since both Christ

---

control over the created order, including the alienated devils, see Patrides, pp. 95-97.

[14] Cedric H. Whitman finds a contrast between Agamemnon and Achilles comparable to what this chapter intends to show in Satan and Christ. Agamemnon is the nadir, as Achilles is the zenith of heroic assumption; he abuses his sceptre, and, instead of a stature to match his assumption, he is "magnificently dressed incompetence, dignity marred by pretension, prowess marred by savagery". *Homer and the Heroic Tradition* (Cambridge, 1958), pp. 157-62.

and Satan appear as martial figures, Satan's role in the guise of a Homeric warrior does not reflect upon the old values so much as define his hollowness within this martial garb. The aspect of martial heroism, therefore, does not identify Satan (although his vices correspond on some points with the old values), nor is it in the nature of a devil's disguise: it is rather an honorable role which his moral position makes it impossible to sustain.

This principle is also found in *Comus*, and it has much the same significance although here the role is clearly a devil's disguise. Comus and the attending spirit are diametrically opposed in their purpose, but they nonetheless appear in the same form, that of shepherd protector and guide: it is a guise hardly more appropriate to the angel who comes to protect the Lady, nor hardly less appropriate to the devil who comes to destroy. In effect, the figure of the Good Shepherd is for the masque or the pastoral what the martial hero is for the epic – a role which manifests those ideals and values conventionally celebrated in the genre. It is devilishly appropriate for Satan to take the form of the noblest, most august figure in the framework in which he appears. The Lady is deceived at first but she has the reason to see that the shepherd is not what he appears to be, and the reader is in much the same position as the Lady; her success in seeing through the devil's disguise is a standard by comparison to which those critics who have traipsed off after the wrong shepherd seem (to the dispassionate observer) more than a little morally exposed.[15]

Satan's heroic role is defined by a number of epic conventions. Like Achilles hurling down the sceptre of Agamemnon,[16] Satan

---

[15] The moral tone of the debate over Milton is pronounced. Douglas Bush, disposing of a group of offenders and heartily certain that the occasion would never arise, declared that he would rather go to hell with a Christian Platonist than to heaven with a naturalistic positivist. "Recent Criticism of Paradise Lost", *PQ*, XXVIII (January, 1949), 31-43. On the other side, William Empson's most recent book, *Milton's God*, consigns to outer darkness all Christian Platonists to begin with.

[16] Whitman notes that hurling down the sceptre is a regular motif whose meaning varies according to the context. When Telemachus does it *(Odyssey* II, p. 280), it signifies his own lack of power and authority. When Achilles hurls Agamemnon's sceptre on the ground, he defies his authority as king *(Iliad* I, 225-47), pp. 160-62.

rejects the regal sceptre of the Son, his king (V, 815-16, 886-87).
Satan arouses his devil legions by appealing not to their cause of
liberty but "what we more affect,/ Honour, Dominion, Glory and
renown" (VI, 419-22). To the Christian standard that the cause
must be just, he opposes the Homeric one that the cause is irrelevant when honor's at the stake: "The strife which thou call'st
evil, but wee style/ The strife of Glory: which we mean to win/
Or turn this Heav'n itself into the Hell/ Thou fablest" (VI, 289-
92). Milton himself follows the epic convention of memorializing
these martial 'deeds of eternal fame' (VI, 240), moving across
the panorama of battle to sing of various exploits:

> Meanwhile in other parts like deeds deserv'd
> Memorial, where the might of Gabriel fought,
> And with fierce Ensigns pierc'd the deep array
> Of Moloch.　　(IV, 354-57)

He describes the devils in conventional epic battle poses. Moloch
faces Gabriel, and, like Achilles, threatens "at his Chariot wheels
to drag him bound". Satan is borne off the field as wounded
Hector was "Back to his Chariot; where it stood retir'd/ From
off the files of war" (VI, 337-39).

Satan's battlefield encounters with warrior angels take the form
of ritual single combats and are accompanied by the custom of
flyting. In primitive epics, skill at arms was accompanied by skill
in boasting, and flyting was an important part of the combat. The
two heroes first battled with words, then, like Marlowe's Tamber-
laine, spoke with the sword to give substance to their threats. It
was a ritual preliminary to a dramatic confrontation in an age
when the battle was a means of winning glory. The warrior who
could daunt his foe with mighty threats was well on his way to
daunting him in battle. He boasted of his lineage, his prowess
and his fighting record, as well as the valor of his comrades, and
he scorned the bravery and skill of his opponent.[17] Satan's battles

---

[17]　Hector taunts Ajax with martial rhetoric (*Iliad* VII, 234-37), and Virgil
follows the formula too. Remulus taunts Ascanius by calling the Phrygians
soft, his own race, hardy: "Yours is embroidered raiment of saffron and
shining sea purple. Indolence is your pleasure, your delight the luxurious
dance; you wear sleeved tunics and ribboned turbans" (*Aeneid* IX, 590-

with Abdiel and Michael feature a flyting match (VI, 131-88) and a confrontation of appropriately heroic proportions. Satan and Michael seem "Fit to decide the Empire of great Heav'n"; when they brandish their weapons, "expectation stood/ In horror", and the angel and devil legions retire in silence to witness the great event (VI, 306-08). Fallen Satan also engages in flyting with Ithuriel and Zephon (IV, 839-40), and Gabriel (IV, 910-60).

By Raphael's process of accommodation, these conventions translate the cosmic conflict into conventional heroic terms: they also give stature and lustre to the antagonist, despite the fact that such attitudes as Homeric honor contradict the heroic standard of the poem. Even in Books I and II, Satan and his rebel legions seem no less heroic in defeat, "highly they raged . . . Hurling defiance toward the Vault of Heav'n" (I, 668-69). Satan is great in size and defiant in the face of odds (I, 97-109). Milton compares his shield to the moon (I, 287) and his spear to a great Norwegian pine (I, 292-93). Like Achilles and Turnus, he acts in "high disdain, from sense of injur'd merit,/ That with the mightiest rais'd me to contend" (I, 98-99). His legions appear in "guise/ Of Warriors old with order'd Spear and Shield", a "Forest huge of Spears: and thronging Helms". Then he marches them out "in perfect *Phalanx* to the Dorian Mood . . . such as rais'd/ To highth of noblest temper Heroes old/ Arming to Battle" (I, 550-53). Moreover, there seems to be good reason for the concern which some have shown at the beauty of Satan's kingdom, and its similarity to heaven.[18] Pandemonium is a golden palace (I, 713-17) comparable to the kingly palace gate on the wall of heaven (III, 506-07). Little wonder, since the architect of pandemonium had built in heaven "many a Tow'red structure high,/ Where Scepter'd Angels held thir residence" (I, 733-34). Satan rules this kingdom "High on a Throne of Royal State", and, like Christ, 'by merit rais'd' to his position. If we take Satan at

---

620). Tasso's pagan champion, Argantes, approaches the Christians with scorn and sarcasm (XI, 61), and begins his battle against Tancred with an extended wit combat.

[18] Bowra, *From Virgil to Milton*, pp. 233-34; Peter, *A Critique of Paradise Lost*, p. 86; Ross, *Poetry and Dogma*, pp. 224-25.

his word, his leadership is based on all of the traditional sanctions – right reason, the law of God, free election, and the eminence of being the greatest warrior:

> Mee though just right, and the fixt Laws of Heav'n
> Did first create your Leader, next, free choice,
> With what besides, in Counsel or in Fight,
> Hath been achiev'd of merit.   (II, 18-21)

The impression of Satan which these conventions convey is unmistakably heroic, and these details are so numerous and well defined that one can only conclude that this was part of Milton's intention. Yet there are also tragic and comic features in this heroic portrait which have much to do with the total impression. The tragic pathos which accompanies the conventional hero's fall and recognition of his fate is only momentarily glimpsed in Milton's Satan, for he spurns repentance and fixes his course toward despair, malice and damnation (the clearest view of the process is seen in VI, 32-113). It is at this point of Satan's anguished recognition of his position that he becomes, and almost at once ceases to be, tragic, for he rejects the repentance to which a reasoned analysis of his position leads him ("O then at last relent" IV, 79), because of disdain and the fear of shame before the devils (IV, 82-83). Perhaps Milton is thinking of Hector whom he cites in the *Reason of Church Government* as an example of one whose noble actions proceed from fear of shame and of tarnishing his reputation:

It was thought of old in philosophy that shame, or to call it better, the reverence of our elders, our brethren, and friends, was the greatest incitement to virtuous deeds and the greatest dissuasion from unworthy attempts that might be. Hence we may read in the *Iliad*, where Hector being wished to retire from the battle, many of his forces being routed, makes answer that he durst not for shame, lest the Trojan knights and dames should think he did ignobly.[19]

Hector's sense of reputation and fear of shame become, in Satan, a mere self-deception.

The self-deception implicit in Satan's crucial choice introduces a comic element. A useful parallel can be found in Lear, who is

[19]   *Works* III, i, 259.

comic in much the same sense as Satan, that is, when a character's conception of himself overreaches what he actually is. The comic sense accompanies self-deceived Lear, blustering and storming to his daughters, "I will do such things – / What they are, yet I know not, but they shall be/ The terrors of the earth" (II, iv). Both Lear and Satan are comic because the circumstances are so clearly different from their perception of them. Lear ceases to be comic as his ordeal teaches him that he is but a 'very foolish, fond old man', but Satan, though his stature diminishes, continues to act as though he were forever the archangel of heavenly spirits. Despite the lesson of the war in heaven, he continues in disobedience, insisting that his is a mind not to be changed by place or time. This is basically a comic situation, but Satan's cosmic misjudgment and calamitous fall produce a special impression. This great figure who contrives to act as he always did is less a fool than a grandly noble grotesque. His defiance is effrontery, his honor vainglory, and his self-sacrifice an illusion. For all the comic possibilities in Satan, he is not a Braggadocchio masquerading in knightly dress, but an anti-hero struggling to retain the heroic lustre he gradually loses. La Rochfoucauld observed that hypocrisy is the homage that vice offers to virtue: Milton recognized this in his creation of Satan.

It is for this reason that the heroic conventions in *Paradise Lost*, despite their grandeur, appear slightly awry on Satan. Milton, for example, makes use of the marvelous – a standard epic element often associated with the hero. A minor marvel is Achilles' talking horse; a more important one is the awe and amazement he arouses in the Trojan forces. The Renaissance generally agreed with Aristotle that the epic should contain the marvelous, though poets and critics insisted on probability as well. Tasso expressed the familiar assumption that the epic has a special way of invoking delight by moving the reader to wonder.[20] In the Christian epic, miraculous transformations and deceptions may be wrought by the devil, but the truly marvelous is saved for the

---

[20] *Discourse*, in Allan H. Gilbert, ed., *Literary Criticism: Plato to Dryden* (New York, 1940), p. 470.

forces of God.[21] Christ's martial aspect strikes the devils with astonishment (VI, 838-39), but his most impressive marvels are the result of his charity and creative power. The account of his victory over Sin and Death strikes wonder into Adam (XII, 467-78); his offer of atonement arouses wonder and awe in the angels (III, 271-73); and the creation of the world is marvelous to Satan (III, 522-23), Uriel (III, 702-04), and Adam (VIII, 10-13). The significant difference between Christ and Satan is partly indicated by the kind of marvels they achieve. Like Archimago, Satan transforms himself into various forms – a cherub, a toad, and a serpent – in order to achieve his ends, but these are petty tricks compared with the works of Christ. In Book I, Milton comments on the kind of marvels achieved by Satan, prefacing his account of the transformation of the infernal council into dwarfs with the mocking intonation, "Behold a wonder!" (I, 777). The scene anticipates the unexpected transformation which overtakes the devil legions in Book X. Both hero and anti-hero perform marvels, but on a different scale and with different results. This kind of disparity between Satan and the heroic standard he presumes to follow is seen in other conventions as well.

On the climactic occasion of Satan's rebellion, it is Abdiel who emerges heroic, not only in facing "Universal reproach, far worse to bear/ Than violence" (VI, 33-35) in the cause of truth, but also in his Promethean isolation, defying Satan and one-third of Heaven ("Flaming Seraph fearless, though alone,/ Encompass'd round with foes" V, 875-76). By both Milton's standard – the warfaring Christian mentioned in *Areopagitica*, who "can apprehend and consider vice with all her baits and seeming pleasures, and yet abstain" – and Satan's standard, Abdiel claims the hero's role.[22] Like Achilles defying Agamemnon and withdrawing

---

[21]   In *Jerusalem Delivered* (I, 17), Godfredo is stricken mute with amazement when God calls him to perform his mission. The beauty of Sophronia is wondrous (II, 21), and were it not for the oncoming night, the poet tells us that Godfredo would have wrought "great wonders" in battle (XI, 82). The charmed rod of Hermes (*Odyssey* XXIV, p. 314) works wonders in the Christian epic too: the charmed rod enables Ubaldo to repel the scaly serpent in Armida's garden (*J.D.* XV, 47-48) and Spenser's Palmer to subdue the wild beasts in the garden of Acrasia (*F.Q.* II, xii, 40).

[22]   For a thorough study of the Abdiel episode in relation to basic themes

from the field over Honor, Abdiel defies Satan and withdraws for
reasons of a truer Honor:

> ... From amidst them forth he pass'd,
> Long way through hostile scorn, which he sustain'd
> Superior, nor of violence fear'd aught;
> And with retorted scorn his back he turned
> On these proud Tow'rs to swift destruction doom'd.
> (V, 903-07)

Although a Norwegian pine is but a wand to Satan's spear, he is
reduced to brandishing it like blind Polyphemus of the *Aeneid*,
as a walking cane "to support uneasy steps/ Over the burning
Marl". In the same vein, Satan's defiant address to his fainting
devil legions has but a 'Semblance of worth, not substance' (I,
529). And since Satan's legions measure all by strength, it is appropriate that they should lose even the spear and shield when
put to the test:

> ... they astonisht all resistance lost,
> All courage; down thir idle weapons dropp'd;
> O'er Shields and Helms, and helmed heads he rode
> Of Thrones and might Seraphim prostrate.
> (VI, 838-41)

Milton also pointedly departs from the epic poet's custom of
praising great exploits. In the pitch of battle in heaven he pauses
to make the important distinction between true and false glory in
order to cut short his account of these deeds:

> I might relate of thousands, and thir names
> Eternize here on Earth; but those elect
> Angels contented with thir fame in Heav'n
> Seek not the praise of men, the other sort
> . . .
> Nameless in dark oblivion let them dwell.
> For strength from Truth divided and from Just,
> Illaudable, naught merits but dispraise
> And ignominy, yet to glory aspires
> Vain-glorious, and through infamy seeks fame:
> Therefore Eternal silence be thir doom.   (VI, 373-85)

---

of the poem, see Mason Tung, "The Abdiel Episode", *SP*, LXII (July,
1965), 595-609.

He earlier invokes the Muse (I, 376) to recount the catalogue of devil leaders because their records have been lost, "blotted out and ras'd/ By thir Rebellion, from the Books of Life" (I, 363). Thus Satan, doomed to will the evil but work the good, now seeks glory, only to gain oblivion.

There is no gainsaying the implausibilities of the war in heaven – the armor worn by angels who would hardly seem to need it, much less be impeded by it; the restricted outcome and duration fixed by God; the fact of a war fought by immortals at all. Milton is aware of it himself, "though strange to us it seem'd/ At first, that Angel should with Angel war" (VI, 91-92). The battle stretches our powers of accommodation to the limits of good sense and beyond, but the pattern is nevertheless firmly grounded on the differences between angelic and demonic that appear so evident elsewhere, and this should make us pause before considering it as "justification for Milton's rejection of war, heroic or chivalric".[23] That the outcome is even until the entrance of Christ is due less to the implication that the sword is useless or a symbol of something farcical or hideous, than to the fact that the demonic legions are in the act of falling, of transforming the sword into a perversion of the power it may represent. It is to be expected that the demonic legions should be almost, but not quite, equal to the angelic powers, because the war is their original disobedience, and God has not yet deprived them of their angelic power:

> . . . sore hath been thir fight,
> As likeliest was, when two such foes met arm'd;
> For to themselves I left them, and thou know'st,
> Equal in their Creation they were form'd,
> Save what sin hath impair'd, which yet hath wrought
> Insensibly, for I suspend thir doom;   (VI, 687-91)

The power which is theirs by virtue of God is still theirs to use against God; otherwise the principle of free will (dramatically defined in Abdiel's choice) evaporates. Satan and his legions do not lose the external power of the sword until they have lost the

---

[23] Helen Gardner, *A Reading of Paradise Lost*, p. 68; see also Summers, *The Muse's Method*, pp. 122ff.

substance of heroic valor, and the war itself is the choice on which that virtue hinges. That God strikes us as a meddling referee ("foreseen . . . and permitted all" VI, 673) is evidence of his permissive will, which allows the full force of rebellion to occur, but nonetheless retains control over the created order, including the demonic legions of Satan.[24] If Satan has not the power to lead a rebellion, he would not rebel in the first place, and his choice in the matter would be meaningless.

Even at this point, the demonic nature of disobedience begins to assert itself: at the outset, in the superiority of the angels in combat, for example, Gabriel's rout of Moloch; second, in the devil's unchivalrous and pernicious choice of weapons on the second day, a strategy which turns a cosmic battle into a lurid farce. When Satan's legions find themselves overmatched, they turn to cannon. Though the idea requires further powers of accommodation for a modern audience to accept, Helen Gardner[25] has pointed out the undeniable relevance of a tradition – seen in both Spenser and Ariosto – that regarded cannon as a devilish engine, the point being that it makes a sham of the chivalric principle by leveling the brave as well as the cowardly, the strong as well as the weak: "Warr seem'd a civil Game/ To this uproar; horrid confusion heapt/ Upon confusion rose." Of course, gunpowder and cannon rendered chivalry obsolete, but it does not follow that Abdiel's principle that "right makes might" was dead as well, least of all to Milton. His focus here is on that principle, and Satan's recourse to cannon is approximately as 'honorable' as Shakespeare's Achilles – also a fraudulent figure – who murders unarmed Hector.

In short, Milton did not make the best of an obsolete convention by depicting it as a farce, but rather focused on the heroic principle that gave chivalry its original dignity – in literature, if

[24] C. A. Patrides reviews the traditional difficulty of reconciling God's permissive Will and his absolute dominion over the created order, including Satan, and concludes that these conflicting claims "may raise more problems that they settle, but at least they manage to combat the pernicious heresy of dualism that an excessive stress on permissive evil would inadvertently introduce", pp. 95-96.

[25] Gardner, pp. 68-70.

not in life. The fact that he presented this conflict as a battle at all indicates his interest in defining the difference between true and false heroic virtue. He might instead have followed Thomas Heywood (*The Hierarchie of the Blessed Angells*, 1635), who allowed the spirits "No Lances, Swords, nor Bombards" but only 'spirituall Armes'. The confrontation went this way:

> *Lucifer*, charg'd with insolence and spleene;
> When nothing but Humilitie was seene,
> And Reuerence towards God, in Michaels brest,
> By which the mighty Dragon he supprest . . .[26]

The point is essentially the same, that obedience will vanquish disobedience, but I suggest that if Milton were truly averse to the sword, he would hardly have presented his angelic legions and Christ in chivalric garb.

Milton develops the same kind of disparity in his description of Pandemonium. The roof of gold (the floor is gold in heaven I, 682) suggests its inverted structure, and other features suggest inorganic, sterile matter – 'veins of liquid fire', 'Bullion dross', and 'massy Ore'; it is but a 'Straw-built Citadel' (I, 773), and the comparison "Not *Babylon*,/ Nor great Alcairo such magnificence/ Equall'd in all thir glories" (I, 717-19) measures its oriental decadence more than its grandeur. The very materials with which it is built are mined from nature's womb in what amounts to a rape of the created order.[27] Mammon supervises the operation:

> . . . by his suggestion taught,
> Ransacked the Centre, and with impious hands
> Rifl'd the bowels of thir mother Earth
> For Treasures better hid.   (*P.L.* I, 685-88)

The city of Satan manifests a well-organized double view but no real ambiguity. Because Satan and his devils do not have the

---

[26] Quoted in Patrides, p. 94.

[27] On the Renaissance view of mining, see Kester Svendsen, *Milton and Science* (Cambridge, Mass., 1956), pp. 120 ff.; Isabel G. MacCaffrey, *Paradise Lost as "Myth"* (Cambridge, Mass., 1959), pp. 160 ff. Milton's description is reminiscent of the abortion imagery by which Spenser describes Mammon's cave (*F.Q.* II, vii, 16-17); W. B. C. Watkins has analyzed the inverted sexual connotations and note of destructive sterility of these passages. *An Anatomy of Milton's Verse* (Baton Rouge, 1955), pp. 73-74.

substance of order or harmony or heroic virtue, they manage only a tenuous hold upon the appearance.

Milton also subtly adapts the battlefield custom of flyting: it serves a double purpose, not only to cast the same uncertain half-light on Satan that we have observed, but also to define important aspects of his position. Although it follows conventional patterns, the flyting in *Paradise Lost* primarily dramatizes a conflict of ideas. It is not a boast of power so much as a debate of reason, in which the false standard of Satan confronts truth in a free and open encounter. The juxtaposition of true and false in direct debate reveals the distortion of Satan's true position. Gabriel ironically reduces Satan's sense of glory by suggesting that his great quest has been but a 'flight from pain' (IV, 921). Satan's retort is the kind of travesty so familiar to Milton's readers in other debates. *L'Allegro* opens by characterizing melancholy as "forlorn/ 'Mongst horrid shapes, and shrieks, and sights unholy", while *Il Penseroso* associates mirth with "vain, deluding joys,/ The brood of folly"; like Comus who sees temperance only as a 'lean and sallow Abstinence', Satan labels Gabriel's obedience to God as servile ease "with songs to hymn his throne,/ And practis'd distances to cringe, not fight", in contrast to his own noble leadership and readiness to hazard all for his people. And Gabriel replies in kind:

> Faithful to whom? to thy rebellious crew?
> Army of Fiends, fit body to fit head;
> . . .
> And thou sly hypocrite, who now wouldst seem
> Patron of liberty, who more than thou
> Once fawn'd, and cring'd, and servilely ador'd
> Heav'n's awful Monarch?   (IV, 952-60)

In the flyting of Satan and Abdiel, Milton defines true liberty and obedience – the important question of duty towards God (V, 809-907; VI, 131-88). Satan questions Abdiel's motives in the best heroic manner, "thou com'st/ Before thy fellows, ambitious to win/ From me some Plume", and he calls Abdiel's obedience to God simply 'sloth', contrasting his own hardy search for glory with Abdiel's preference for the pleasure of feast and song. But Abdiel defines for him the basis of true obedience:

> God and Nature bid the same,
> When he who rules is worthiest, and excels
> Them whom he governs.   (VI, 176-78)

In their exchange in Book V, Abdiel replies to Satan's rejection of obedience as 'knee-tribute ... prostration vile' with the unanswerable point, "Shalt thou give Law to God, shalt thou dispute/ With him the points of liberty, who made/ Thee what thou art?" (V, 822-24). Abdiel quits the flyting match and the rebel legions when Satan, losing all reason, argues the ultimate presumption, rejection of his Maker: "We know no time when we were not as now;/ Know none before us, self-begot, self-rais'd/ By our own quick'ning power." By putting to use the flyting convention, Milton is able to define dramatically the debate of reason upon which depends the outcome of the battle of arms.

Milton creates an interesting variation on a flyting match in Homer when Satan encounters Death (II, 672-734). In the *Iliad* (VI, 119-236) Glaukos, a Trojan warrior, encounters Diomedes on the battlefield, and they engage in the customary flyting match. They are unknown to one another; thus Diomedes is prudent, carefully estimating his opponent for fear that he might be a heavenly spirit in disguise: "But if you are some one of the immortals come down from the bright sky,/ know that I will not fight against any god of the heaven." Diomedes is properly cautious because he knows the story of fierce Lykourgos, the son of Dryas, who "tried to fight with the gods of the bright sky", and came to an unfortunate end. Diomedes recounts Lykourgos's ill-fated assault on Dionysius (VI, 127-32), which angered the gods: "the son of Kronos struck him to blindness, nor did he live long afterwards, since he was hated by all the immortals". Diomedes has been warned by Athene not to fight against the gods (V, 818-21), and he knows that even the offspring of the gods were favored, hence dangerous to attack. Achilles himself is extremely hazardous to meet in battle because he is the favored offspring of a goddess, "it is not for any man to fight with Achilles. There is always some one of the gods with him to beat death from him" (XX, 97). This concern of Diomedes about heavenly spirits is in the background of Milton's scene.

Satan and Death approach one another in the best heroic manner, threatening destruction and insulting the foe: "and now great deeds/ Had been achiev'd, whereof all Hell had rung" (II, 722). Diomedes' prudence about heavenly spirits now appears in Satan as a bold threat to his opponent, "Retire, or taste thy folly, and learn by proof,/ Hell-born, not to contend with Spirits of Heav'n" (II, 685-86). As a recently fallen heavenly spirit, his warning is thus a measure of his presumption that he is still the archangel spirit of heaven. In his rebellion against God, Satan has gone over the brink with Lykourgos, but he now speaks as though nothing has changed, as though he were still one of the heavenly hierarchy. Death challenges such a threat with a rhetorical question that cuts to the heart of Satan's presumption: "Art thou that Traitor Angel ... And reck'nst thou thy self with Spirits of Heav'n/ Hell-doomd ...?" At this point, Satan develops some necessary prudence of his own. Death is king and lord now, and Sin warns Satan that not even he can resist Death's terrible dart.

A second element of travesty lies in their kinship and reconciliation. Glaukos proudly traces his lineage, not only to reassure Diomedes that he is indeed mortal, but also to offer his credentials and boast of his proud family line. Their encounter ends in an unexpected reconciliation; the two heroes embrace when Diomedes discovers that they are 'guests and friends from the days of ... [their] fathers' (VI, 231). Satan and Death reach an accord too, despite the fact that Death is to his father a 'sight ... detestable'. They are interrupted by Sin who points out that they are long-lost kin, in fact, father and son. Thus Glaukos's proud and lengthy elaboration of his lineage is developed here into travesty, as Sin relates at great length (727-814), and in rather embarrassingly specific detail, the lineage which these two heroes share. The incest and rape by which this lineage has developed is anything but honorable, in fact, the kind of lineage which a battlefield hero would blush to acknowledge. Thus Milton arranges a bizarre reconciliation out of standard heroic themes – lineage, flyting, and Diomedes' reluctance to do battle with heavenly spirits.

The contrast between hero and anti-hero which Milton presents through these battlefield conventions is continued in the larger conventions of the council and journey. In Homer, the council is limited to heroes: it is a mark of honor to sit down in the company of brave warriors and decide what course to follow. When Achilles withdraws from the field, he withdraws from the council as well, "Never now would he go to assemblies where men win glory" (I, 490). And his affront to Agamemnon takes the form of refusing to join him either in the council or in action (IX, 374). Lowly Thersites learns what it means to speak up in a council where he does not belong; Odysseus beats him from the assembly for chiding Agamemnon,[28] for presuming to argue with princes (II, 248-51). Odysseus' particular greatness is that he is, like Nestor, wise in council. The two of them bring caution and amity to an often tumultuous assembly, and cement unity among the leaders. The wise advice of the great counsellor is something the hero risks disaster in ignoring. Agamemnon is humbled when he disregards Nestor's advice to placate Achilles, and Hector is doomed when he forgets the sage advice of Polydamus to stay within the walls of Troy.

In the council scenes, Homer delineates the individual qualities of his heroes. As each speaks his mind in the council, he reveals his motives, his strengths and weaknesses. The council also reveals latent conflicts and generally reflects the state of affairs in the body politic. The hierarchy becomes defined as each hero speaks in turn, and as the assembly heeds or ignores what he advises. The discord in Agamemnon's army, for example, is dramatized in the first council scene. Nestor steps between the feuding heroes to caution Agamemnon not to claim Briseis, and Achilles, not to match his strength with the king's. But Agamemnon disregards his advice, and the two heroes, "after battling in words of contention stood up, and broke the assembly" (I, 304-05). The second council dramatizes Agamemnon's lost authority and prestige,[29] and the discordant results of Achilles' withdrawal. The

[28] Thersites here provides a low parallel to Achilles. But Thersites has no right to chide and is whipped out of the assembly with the sceptre which Achilles earlier has cast down (II, 265-69). Odysseus says Thersites is out of place, and he exercises his authority to reassert order and rank.
[29] As a symbol of Agamemnon's authority, the sceptre, in the hands of

Greeks are deceived by the false dream Zeus sends to Agamemnon. Their extended preparations are fruitless and the attack doomed to failure. Agamemnon's strategy to test his forces' loyalty fails when they take him at his word and run to the ships (II, 142-54). Thersites intrudes in the assembly, and the gods do not accept the Greeks' oblation (II, 419). The fate of the doomed Trojans is also reflected in a crucial council scene. Achilles finally appears on the battlements and is ready to storm the walls, but yields to Odysseus, in the Greek council, and rests his men instead. By contrast, the doomed Trojans, follow Hector instead of Polydamus, and, like Milton's devils responding to the arguments of Mammon (II, 285-92), appear a mob of cheering fools:

So spoke Hector, and the Trojans thundered to hear him; fools, since Pallas Athene had taken away the wits from them. They gave their applause to Hector in his counsel of evil, but none to Polydamus, who had spoken good sense before them. (XVIII, 310-13)

The council scene, particularly the infernal council, is a set piece in the Christian narrative tradition,[30] and frequently serves the same purpose as the Homeric council. Observing the time-honored principle that a figure is revealed through what he says and does, Tasso expresses in his council scenes a sharp contrast between the forces of Godfredo and those of the Turks. In Book I, Tasso's version of venerable Nestor, Peter the Hermit, unites the Christian forces under Godfredo (I, 29-33). The Christian council ends in concord, the sun rises, and Tasso then delivers a catalog of the forces of virtue (I, 35 ff.), following the example of the *Iliad* (II) and the *Aeneid* (X). In contrast, Satan's trumpet summons an infernal council which meets in darkness and tumult, and ends 'with ghastly roar'. Tasso's infernal council displays the

---

others, is a mockery to him. Achilles repudiates him with it (I, 225-47), and Odysseus symbolically assumes his office with it, first to restore order to the battle (II, 185-86), then to unite the assembly (II, 265-76).

[30] Burton Kurth notes that the infernal council was a conventional part of the hexameral tradition, and also in such diverse works as Fletcher's *Apollyonists*, Vida's *Christiad*, Fletcher's *Purple Island*, Crashaw's translation from Marion, *The Suspicion of Herod*, and Cowley's *Davideis. Milton and Christian Heroism*, p. 46.

appropriate qualities of disorder, violence, magniloquence, cowardice and impotence before the power of God.

The same contrasts between heavenly and infernal councils in *Paradise Lost* have long been noticed.[31] The councils exhibit the most significant qualities of hero and anti-hero – Christ's obedience and Satan's pride. The heavenly council is quiet, plain, simple, and unstaged. The infernal council proceeds in oriental pomp with Satan seated above (II, 1-5); it takes place in the inner chambers with only the chieftains present (I, 792); it begins with great fanfare and ostentation (750-59); and it proceeds to a conclusion already decided by Satan (I, 659-62; II, 379-80). Moreover, both Tasso and Milton characterize the Satanic forces through the same infernal types. In Book X, Tasso's Soliman is awakened by Ismen the wizard and conducted to an infernal council in the underworld (X, 34-36). Argantes speaks first, like Moloch, a blunt warlike figure who urges war, "To win with honor, or to die with praise"; he considers the matter simply, "Thus much Argantes said, and said no more/ (As if the case were clear of which he spoke)" (X, 39). In contrast, Orcanes speaks next, like Belial, a smooth and subtle speaker who indirectly implies (because he dare not speak it openly) that they should sue for peace because no one can withstand Godfredo (*J.D.* X, 48). But Ismen answers this cowardice and advises war (X, 49-52); like Beelzebub, he is persuasive ("Dumb stood the knights, so dreadful was his word" X, 52), and he punctures the illusion that the devils have any option between peace and war, proposing only the hopeless and devilish plan of Satan. As one might expect, Tasso's Satan closely resembles Milton's. The remembrance of former glory makes his position unbearable (IV, 10), but he is defiant (IV, 15). He has a sense of injured merit, "Expulsed were with injurious arms,/ From those due honors us of right belong" (IV, 12). His strategy is typically Satanic, "Use open force, or secret guile unspied;/ For craft is virtue, 'gainst a foe defied" (IV, 16).

[31]   See Stein, *Answerable Style*, pp. 38-51; Irene Samuel, "The Dialogue in Heaven: A Reconsideration of *Paradise Lost*, III, 1-417", *PMLA*, LXXII (1957), 601-11; B. Rajan, *Paradise Lost: The Seventeenth Century Reader* (London, 1947), pp. 46-48.

These details and many more sufficiently denote a contrast between the forces of virtue and vice if the reader distinguishes between magnificence and magniloquence, power and violence, harmony and noise. But other important aspects of this moral contrast are apparent only if the reader knows what they ordinarily mean in the tradition Milton draws into the poem. The Homeric council as a ritual gathering of heroes, an appropriate ceremonial setting where the greatest undertake to carry out the plans of the council, is the atmosphere which prevails in Milton's council scenes. In the heavenly council, Christ takes upon himself the task which all others fear – the atonement – and thus assumes the hero's role. When God asks for a volunteer, even the angels are silent, hesitating before the consequences of such a mission:

> He ask'd, but all the Heav'nly Quire stood mute,
> And silence was in Heav'n: on man's behalf
> Patron or Intercessor none appear'd,
> Much less that durst upon his own head draw
> The deadly forfeiture, and ransom set.   (III, 217-221)

Christ has no more foreknowledge than Satan. The confidence with which he undertakes the task is but an expression of his faith and obedience. He is in the classic position of the magnanimous hero who gives up everything in order to gain everything, and without the certainty of gaining it. The solemn occasion then centers upon the Son as he accepts the humiliation of the great task. His offer strikes the angels with admiration, and wins him heavenly glory. It is here that he proves his merit and establishes his birthright as Son of God, his right to the kingdom:

> . . . all Power
> I give thee, reign for ever, and assume
> Thy Merits; under thee as Head Supreme
> Thrones, Princedoms, Powers, Dominions I reduce.
>   (III, 317-20)

Like the new Troy, Christ's kingdom is to be greater than the old; it is to be nothing less than the return of the golden age. The council ends with a hymn of praise for the Son who has become the hero.

86

The infernal council is no less impressive in its ceremony, and it manifests many of the same conventions. Like God, Satan asks "whom shall we send,/ In search of this new world, whom shall we find sufficient?" (II, 402-04). This mission seems to demand great abilities and endurance. The one who is chosen must have the cunning and courage of Odysseus; he is responsible for the welfare of the entire underworld (II, 413-16). Milton touches up the Homeric qualities of the scene (II, 417-29): the devils are 'Champions' but they stand mute at the thought of the 'perilous attempt'; then the greatest of them steps out with Achillean magnanimity, "With Monarchal pride/ Conscious of highest worth", to assume the task. This heroic impression of Satan continues in his acknowledgement of the principle that hazards as well as honors belong to the one who reigns (II, 450-54). Like the angels, the devils award this valor with the highest praise, "as a God/ Extol him equal to the highest in Heav'n", because he has acted for the public weal. His undertaking also seems to involve great sacrifice, "for the general safety he despis'd/ His own" (II, 480-82). The devil leaders then emerge from their inner council in hierarchical order, in 'pomp supreme', and to the sound of the trumpet.

The whole effect, however, is grandiose rather than grand. Satan is but going through the motions of heroic activity. It is immediately noticed in his peculiar prudence, like Achilles, jealous of the honor to be gained:

> ... Thus saying rose
> The Monarch, and prevented all reply,
> Prudent, lest from his resolution rais'd
> Others among the chief might offer now
> (Certain to be refus'd) what erst they fear'd;
> And so refus'd might in opinion stand
> His Rivals, winning cheap the high repute
> Which he through hazard huge must earn.
>
> (II, 466-73)

But Satan hazards nothing, for he has nothing to lose; the hazard of his journey is as ambiguous as his eminence in hell; he is the greatest in being the worst. Satan is assured of a loyal following

in hell because to overleap him would paradoxically be a step
downwards:

> . . . where there is then no good
> For which to strive, no strife can grow up there
> From Faction; for none sure will claim in Hell
> Precedence.   (II, 30-33)

The same effect is observed at the conclusion of the council,
when the devils engage in games and sports (II, 521-628), like
the heroes of old in the fortunate woodlands of the underworld
(*Aeneid* VI, 637 ff.). While the heavenly council ends in solemn
adoration and harps 'ever tun'd', the infernal council ends in a
'deaf'ning shout', and, instead of harmony, there are various forms
of discord. The devils hold games ("Part curb thir fiery Steeds,
or shun the Goal/ With rapid wheels"), but the games become
so violent that hell scarce can hold the 'wild uproar'; the milder
sort turn to the harp, but instead of hymns of adoration, they
sing "thir own Heroic deeds . . . and complain that Fate/ Free
Virtue should enthrall to Force or Chance" (II, 546-51). There
is a semblance of harmony but the substance of their song is a
false complaint. Another group of devils retire to reason high
philosophy; though they are able to "charm pain for a while",
their discourse ultimately is "Vain wisdom all, and false Philoso-
phie", and they find "no end, in wand'ring mazes lost" (II,
557-69).

The most important difference between the hero and anti-hero,
however, lies in the nature of their quest. Christ and Satan both
go on a journey. It is a major motif of the poem and reveals
much about Milton's design. The journey is one of the most enduring myths and at the same time a tangible literary context with
conventions of its own. What are the chief features of the epic
journey, and how does Milton use them? In Book I of the *Iliad*,
Achilles contemptuously asks Agamemnon "how shall any one of
the Achaians readily obey you either to go on a journey or to
fight men strongly in battle?" (I, 150-51). His taunt suggests
that the journey, like the battlefield, and the council, was an important part of a hero's role. Most great epics embody the journey
and some form of the formula of the rites of passage: separation,

initiation, and return.[32] Milton himself describes the mythic pattern in Christian terms:

> After wandering about upon the earth for some time, like some heavenly visitant, in holiness and righteousness, [man's] spirit was to take its flight upward to the heaven whence it had come and to return once more to the abode and home which was its birthright.[33]

The great literary models for the quest in the Western tradition were Odysseus' journey home and Aeneas' journey to find a new Troy. Christian poets found in them the essential pattern for the Christian journey.

The journey is a test of hardships placed in the way of the hero who has become separated or lost. His quest is an attempt to regain some form of lost bliss, the memory of which sharpens his sense of present grief. The familiar predicament is described by the Anglo-Saxon *Wanderer*:

> But the friendless man awakes, and he sees the yellow waves,
> And the sea-birds dip to the sea, and broaden their wings
> [to the gale,
> And he sees the dreary rime, and the snow commingled
> [with hail.
> O, then are the wounds of his heart the sorer much for this,
> The grief for the loved and lost made new by the dream
> [of old bliss.[34]

In both the *Odyssey* and the *Aeneid*, the hero is an outcast wanderer, a 'neighborless man' facing the elements alone.[35] Aeneas is "unknown, destitute, driven from Europe and Asia, to wander the Libyan wilderness" (*Aeneid* I, 384-85). In Book III, he recounts the beginning of the voyage in this way: "we were driven by divine omens to seek distant places of exile in wastelands . . . weeping I leave the shores and havens of my country, and the plains where once was Troy. I sail to sea an exile" (III, 4-11).

---

[32] Joseph Campbell finds this myth of deeds and heroes in all cultures. *The Hero With a Thousand Faces* (New York, 1949), p. 4.

[33] *Private Correspondence and Academic Exercises*, trans. P. B. Tillyard, ed. E. M. W. Tillyard (Cambridge, 1932), p. 107.

[34] *Select Translations from Old English Poetry*, eds. Albert S. Cook and Chauncey B. Tinker (New York, 1902).

[35] For example, *Odyssey* V, p. 83, VI, p. 90; *Aeneid* V, 626-29.

Life in a primitive society doubtless accounts in large measure for the prominence of the motif. In a primitive society, the circle of family and friends, the protection of the clan and the bond of the comitatus were most important: the alternative of lonely banishment was invoked only as a strong punishment. Young Telemachus, on his own journey, encounters a stranger, Theoclymenus, who for killing a kinsman, fled the death sentence to a doom almost as grim: "I fled their dark sentence of death, thereby dooming myself to wander across the habitable world" (*Odyssey* XV, p. 215). He is a fugitive, pursued by avengers, and his life is never safe. It is, as Odysseus tells Eumeus, 'the saddest of human fates'. On such a journey, the hero inevitably gets lost. Odysseus and his men, unable to distinguish light from darkness, wander into Circe's island wood of error (X, p. 141). Aeneas and his men even lose their guide, Palinurus, and experience what it means to be truly lost – the unreality of existing in a dimensionless void and of dreading the unknown without guidance or a sense of order.[36]

To make matters worse, the hero is also plagued by an angry god, often unjustly and without reason. Odysseus must seek refuge from cruel Poseidon (V, pp. 77-80), and Aeneas is tormented by vindictive Juno ("Is anger so fierce in celestial spirits?"), although she knows that his ultimate success is certain. Of course the Christian approximation of Juno is Satan, the ruler of darkness who plagues man. Thus the situation is often grim, but the hero is at least sustained in his exile by the prophecy of success. Zeus decrees that Odysseus shall finally return home, and, Athene also protects Telemachus, warning him to make a journey in preparation for Odysseus' return. Aeneas has the same kind of protection in Venus, who sees that Jupiter keeps his promises (I, 228-79), and his exile is marked by a number of favorable omens – a shooting star from Jupiter (II, 692-98), Creusa's ghost (II, 776-84), Anchises' vision of the future (VI, 752-898), and the ghost of Hector.

---

[36] Campbell describes the mythic hero moving in a "dream landscape of curiously fluid, ambiguous forms, where he must survive a succession of trials". p. 97.

A melange of perils and temptations which tempted the cunning and courage of Odysseus had enough fascination to become traditional. Odysseus is stranded and encouraged to remain in bliss with beautiful Calypso, a motif which is repeated in the magnificent grove of Athene, the garden of Alcinous' palace. Odysseus and his men resist the lotosflower and the Sirens, outwit the Cyclops, and escape from the Laestrygonians, only to turn loose the fierce winds of Aeolus, and Circe detains them for a year "sitting to table and delighting in her untold wealth of flesh and mellow wine" (X, p. 148). (Aeneas too is a year with Dido in Carthage) Virgil tests Aeneas with similar perils in his search for the destined land. He must flee the plain of Mavors (III, 13-61) and the Strophades (III, 209-69), and avoid King Anius (III, 84-98); pestilence and death strike his people at Crete (III, 137-39), but, warned in advance, Aeneas avoids the island of Cyclope's cave and the straits of Scylla and Charybdis (III, 558-686).

An important part of the journeys of both Odysseus and Aeneas is the visit to the underworld. Mythic heroes take a night journey into the depths of the earth or into the sea to bring back the secrets of the deep for benefit of man, and for a more complete understanding of the self. Odysseus and Aeneas enter the underworld to seek knowledge of themselves, to learn the future, and to see the promised end. In the Christian tradition it is a paradoxical descent into the darkness to find the light of wisdom. Saint Augustine advised "Descend that you may ascend", and Christ's descent furnished Christians with a model for descending into darkness in order to ascend in triumph to the light.[37] The wanderer acquired wisdom when his external eye was darkened so that the inner eye would see. By the same token, Odysseus must consult blind Tiresias to learn the 'threads of destiny woven in the gods' design'.

In Virgil's hell, Aeneas learns that the promised land is not to be gained without a struggle. Sybil tells him what Dante and other Christian voyagers were to learn, that "easy is the descent

[37] Don Cameron Allen, "Milton and the Descent to Light", *JEGP*, LX (1961), 614-30.

into hell ... but to recall thy steps ... this is the task, this the burden" (VI, 890-92). Creusa's ghost tells Aeneas "thou shalt come to the land Hesperia, where Lydian Tiber flows with soft current through rich and populous fields" (II, 781-82), but he finds that the quest is only half over once he reaches it. Turnus is there to be reckoned with, and Aeneas must therefore fight his own battle of Troy once the odyssey is finished. This feature of the hero's journey is also prominent in the *Odyssey*: Odysseus returns home in disguise to find a household corrupted with false servants and preying suitors. Carefully distinguishing the loyal from the disloyal, the true from the false, he slaughters the suitors, garrots the false serving maids, hangs treacherous Melanthius, and completes the task with a fire of purification (XXII, pp. 299-304).

These details of the classical journey – the search for a lost bliss, the outcast wanderer lost in darkness, the hostile god, the promise of return, monstrous perils and temptations cast in the way of the hero, the visit to the underworld, and the Hesperian garden at the end of the quest – were all readily adaptable to the voyage of the Christian. Odysseus purifying his household, for example, readily illustrated an important Christian idea: the corrupt garden paradise was a symbol of sin and imperfection which the Christian knight must purify or overcome once he has found it. Guyon destroys Acrasia's garden paradise and Rinaldo conquers Jerusalem. The sacred garden is ruled by a demon temptress, and the holy city is occupied by pagan infidels. As Raphael tells Adam, "So little knows/ Any, but God alone to value right/ The good before him, but perverts best things/ To worst abuse, or to this meanest use" (*P.L.* IV, 201-04). The perversion of the garden symbolizes all of the other implications of the fall: love, honor, reason, obedience, and beauty are corrupted but continue to wear the brows of grace. The divine love of charity has become, in the false garden, the self-love of cupidity. As Spenser says, "when the world woxe old",

> Then beautie which made to represent
> The great Creatours owne resemblance bright
> Unto abuse of lawlesse lust was lent,

And made the baite of bestiall delight:
Then faire grew foule, and foule grew faire in sight.

(*F.Q.* IV, viii, 32)

The journeys of both Redcrosse and Guyon illustrate this symbolism, and borrow many features of the journey of Odysseus. Imagery of a weather-beaten ship on a storm-tossed sea [38] describes the progress of Guyon, the wayfaring Christian, traveling through desolate and barren country (II, vii, 2). The homeric monsters and birds of prey which he encounters signify specifically Christian forms of temptation and danger. Homer's Charybdis is now the gulf of greediness, which Guyon avoids by steering a straight and narrow course behind his palmer, reason (II, xii, 2). Opposite, the peril of Scylla becomes for Guyon the 'rock of reproch', the fate of 'wanton joyes and lustes intemperate'. Guyon, like Odysseus, must avoid the false havens: the wandering islands which seem to be a firm haven of rest, but which "have ofte drawne many a wandring wight/ Into most deadly daunger and distressed plight" (II, xii, 11); the allure of wanton Phaedria (II, xii, 14-17); the siren melodies of mermaids; the whirlpool of decay, sea monsters, and the forgeries of the woeful maiden (II, xii, 18-30). Guyon also wanders in a fog so dark that not even his palmer can find the way (II, xii, 35-39), and he must play the warfaring Christian once he reaches the Hesperian garden, uprooting the temptress Acrasia. Redcrosse is a lonely wanderer in a dark, confusing wood of error – the lost Christian soul trying to find his way to Grace. Spenser readily assimilates the malicious god of Virgil and Homer, who tries to prevent the completion of the journey: Archimago tries every means to divert Redcrosse, but the knight's own steadfastness and the intervention of Arthur assure Archimago's failure. In marrying Una and freeing her captive parents from the dragon, Redcrosse symbolically regains from man his lost paradise.

In *Paradise Lost*, the subject itself is the story of how Adam and Eve sired a race of wanderers, and of why every man since the fall is on his own journey of exile. The journey of the way-

---

[38]　*Faerie Queene* II, ii, 24; II, vii, 1; II, xii, 1.

faring and warfaring Christian epitomizes the predicament of man, and, as one would expect, the journey motif is seen in Adam after the fall. As for Christ and Satan, Christ's role in both epics is the original pattern for which other literary Christian quests are allegories. Consequently, the conventional details of the allegorical journeys of Tasso and Spenser's knights were conveniently at hand for Milton to use with Christ, the untried, young hero. Milton then employs the same details of the journey in his characterization of Satan, whose moral position as fallen hero is defined through the imagery of exiled wanderer. Thus the journey motif expresses the same contrast of hero and anti-hero as do the conventions of battlefield and council, defining the rise of the young hero and the fall of the once-mighty antagonist.

As in the council and on the battlefield, the inner spirit of Christ's virtue undergirds his heroic journey. Moses leading the Israelites to the promised land was an Old Testament type of the redemption, and Milton seems to emphasize the role. Heroic Aeneas leading his people from the ruins of Troy is also in the background; Adam learns that Christ will bring back "Through the world's wilderness long wander'd man/ Safe to eternal Paradise of rest" (XII, 310-14). Christ also destroys the old corrupted order: it is prophesied that a new Paradise, like Troy, shall rise from the ashes of the old (III, 333-37), an image which reappears in Michael's vision of the new kingdom:

> ... to dissolve
> *Satan* with his perverted World, then raise
> From the conflagrant mass, purg'd and refin'd,
> New Heav'ns, new Earth, Ages of endless date.
>   (XII, 546-49)

There are other parallels to Aeneas in the imagery of Christ's desolate journey in *Paradise Regained*. As we have seen, he is an untried youth whose promise is yet to be tested. God tests his steadfastness and obedience in the wilderness before sending him to battle Satan: "There he shall lay down his rudiments/ Of his great warfare, e're I send him forth/ To conquer Sin and Death" (*P.R.* I, 157-59). Christ's progress in the desert resembles Aeneas' journey into the underworld: he enters the "bordering Desert wild,/ And with dark shades and rocks environ'd round" (I, 193-94) in order to 'learn and know' what the future will hold and how he must accomplish his task.

Satan's journey is an elaborate parallel to the great epic journeys. As leader of the fallen angels, Satan undertakes the deliverance of his people from defeat and misery ("while I abroad/ Through all the Coasts of dark destruction seek/ Deliverance for us all" II, 463-65).[39] He fosters their hopes that by chance they may "Re-enter Heav'n; or else in some mild zone/ Dwell not unvisited of Heav'n's fair Light" (II, 397-400), that they may at last arrive at the 'happy Isle'. The new land has been foretold to Satan just as it was to Aeneas (III, 345-48). By Satan's testimony, his journey ends in triumph; the devils will "possess, as Lords, a spacious World" (X, 466), and a new empire will be created for his lost offspring, Sin and Death. In fact, Satan's return is a subtle parody of the convention of the hero's lineage. Sin and Death, 'his Offspring dear', recognize him and praise his great deeds, his "Wisdom gain'd/ With odds what War hath lost", and Satan replies grandly that he has established for them a proud name:

> Fair Daughter, and thou Son and Grandchild both,
> High proof ye now have giv'n to be the Race
> Of *Satan* (for I glory in the name,
> Antagonist of Heav'n's Almighty King)
> Amply have merited of me, of all
> Th' Infernal Empire . . .
> . . .
> All yours, right down to Paradise descend,
> There dwell and Reign in bliss.   (X, 384-99)

Like Aeneas and Odysseus, Satan fulfills his duty toward his son and heirs, establishing their birthright once again.

Thus both Christ and Satan go on a journey and both achieve glory in the council by undertaking it; but as Spenser says, "gold al is nat, that doth golden seeme,/ Ne all good knights, that shake well speare and shield" (II, viii, 14). Although his journey resembles Christ's in many of its features, he ultimately represents

---

[39] See also *P.L.* IV, 938-40; *P.R.* I, 112-18.

a different model – the defeated sinner who has fallen from grace and been cast into outer darkness. If Christ emerges from the heavenly council (the 'Courts of everlasting Day') to descend into the 'darksome House of mortal Clay' of man, in sacrificial atonement, Satan hopes to ascend, and his purpose is manifestly unheroic, his journey but another example of "falsehood under saintly show,/ Deep malice to conceal, couch't with revenge" (IV, 121-23).

In Satan's journey the heroic pattern is reversed, even to the paradox itself. Satan claims that the fall into hell is also explained by the paradox, "From this descent/ Celestial Virtues rising, will appear/ More glorious and more dread than from no fall" (II, 14-16), but it is hardly the same thing. Their descent has been made not in humble obedience but in cosmic pride. And his journey out of hell is a desperate ascent away from the self-knowledge that comes when the epic hero descends into darkness. It is an ascent toward light, but the spirit of his quest – to overcome Adam and corrupt the garden – further alienates him from God and the light of truth, and he sinks deeper into spiritual darkness and exile. In contrast to Christ in the wilderness relying upon God for guidance, Satan appeals to the spirits of chaos (II, 973-76). And as for the monsters and perils he encounters, in hell itself are all the 'Gorgons, and Hydras and Chimeras dire' with which Homer populated the infernal world. The Scylla and Charybdis of Satan's voyage are Sin and Death at the narrow gates of hell. Like Aeneas (Aeneid VI, 273-89), Satan finds the gates guarded, but these monsters, symbolizing the hell within of the Christian exile, are Satan's own. In the normal pattern of the Christian journey, the hero overcomes the perils in his path by first subduing his own inner chamber of horrors – the doubts, fears, despair, and pride of the unregenerate. But there is no inner triumph in Satan, and he continues to travel in the shadow of Cain, an outcast vagabond whose isolation, darkness, and uncertainty are symptoms of his spiritual darkness within. Though he goes through the motions of heroic savior of his people in the pattern of Aeneas, Satan's moral position establishes a new pattern: like Theoclymenus in the *Odyssey*, he is a doomed outcast. There are thus two distinct journeys Adam can follow, depending upon the wisdom of his choices.

The climax of Satan's journey and of the earlier council scenes is the elaborate scene of his return to the infernal council (X, 427-545). It is an important climax to Satan's role in the poem, a fitting conclusion to the ironic manner in which his pride and malice have been hitherto presented. The paraphernalia of the heroic leader is elaborate. The devils keep watch around their city for the return of their 'great Adventurer' (X, 440). After a triumphant return, Satan ascends his high throne in triumph sitting in 'regal lustre', like God in a cloud.[40] His presumption and magnificence are exaggerated further in the form of address he employs: "Thrones, Dominations, Princedoms, Virtues, Powers" (X, 460), like God addressing the angelic hierarchy – the nine ranks of Seraphim, Cherubim, Thrones, Dominations, Virtues, Powers, Principalities, Archangels and Angels.[41] Beelzebub earlier uses this form of address conditionally, "or these Titles now/ Must we renounce, and changing style be call'd/ Princes of Hell?" (II, 310-13). But now Satan assumes the titles by right of his successful voyage, and misses the irony in the phrase "Successful beyond hope":

> Thrones, Dominations, Princedoms, Virtues, Powers,
> For in possession such, not only of right,
> I call ye and declare ye now, returned
> Successful beyond hope, to lead ye forth
> Triumphant.   (X, 460-64)

It is another measure of Satan's presumption that he should speak as though the devils are essentially unchanged, but the reader sees in these details a radical dislocation of form and

---

[40] Cf. *Iliad* I, 359. The Bible also provides precedent which Milton follows directly in XII, 201-04. In Exodus 13:21, God appears before the Israelites in the form of a cloud by day and pillar of fire by night. Elsewhere in *Paradise Lost* God appears as a presence, hidden in a cloud of brightness: III, 375-80; IV, 597; V, 598-99, 642-43; VI, 27-28, 56-59; X, 32. To deliver God's judgment of Adam, Michael appears in a cloud (XI, 865); and in Michael's prophecy of the future, Christ is seen "last in the Clouds from Heav'n to be reveal'd", to destroy Satan's world.

[41] See also *P.L.* III, 319-20; V, 600-02; X, 86-88; XI, 296-98.

spirit, and his magnificent appearance in this council scene is only thinly sustained. Satan's humor is that of a condemned man:

> . . . Him by fraud I have seduc'd
> From his Creator, and the more to increase
> Your wonder, with an Apple; he thereat
> Offended, worth your laughter, hath giv'n up
> Both his beloved Man and all his World.
>
> (X, 485-90)

He is now less able to sustain a heroic appearance – hence his more exaggerated efforts to maintain the pose. Like Vanity getting older, the deeper he falls into sin, the more vigorous and frantic are his efforts to sustain the illusion of heroic virtue. As the successful voyager-hero, he describes his mythic 'journey strange' where he learned the secrets of the 'new created World'. Like Odysseus or Beowulf, Satan recounts his deeds and the great perils he has undergone, "Long were to tell/ What I have done, what suffer'd, with what pain/ Voyag'd th' unreal, vast, unbounded deep" (X, 469-71). He recounts the 'new created World' that he has, in his words, purchased 'with a bruise', and then commands his people "up and enter now into full bliss" (X, 500-03).

The unexpected result of this exaggerated regal council is the end toward which Satan's heroism has been leading from the beginning. Seeing Satan in a star-bright cloud reminds us of Satan in Book IX, creeping about darkly, "thus wrapt in mist/ Of midnight vapour", and finally descending into a "beast, and mixt with bestial slime" (IX, 158-65). Satan vainly supposes that he is untouched by the evil he performs, that his mind can surmount place and time, and that his fine appearance will continue to reflect the heavenly spirit he once was. But he finds that he becomes what he does, that his spirit changes as he becomes hardened in sin, and that his appearance changes with his spirit.[42]

Satan has gradually lost his ability to effect disguises. In his cherubic disguise in Eden, his inward torments "marr'd his borrow'd visage, and betray'd/ Him counterfeit" (IV, 116-17). Then

---

[42] Isabel Gamble MacCaffrey, *Paradise Lost as "Myth"* (Cambridge, Mass., 1959), pp. 64-73.

he is insulted when Ithuriel does not recognize him "in his own shape" (IV, 823-30), and when Gabriel sees him of "Regal port/ But faded splendor wan" (IV, 869-70). After he has descended into brutish form to tempt Eve, he is not easily able to resume the angelic appearance, for Sin and Death immediately see through his disguise of 'an Angel bright' (IX, 327-31). In the climactic scene of Satan's return, it seems that he has discarded his bestial disguise and resumed his angelic form, but the scene discovers him hollow. Far from degrading Satan, Milton here returns to the elegance and defiance Satan has exhibited in Books I-II in order to show that spirit ultimately determines form in Satan as well. Both Satan and the devils are punished "in the shape he sinn'd" (X, 516). The heroic forms which Satan has assumed now fall away, and the triumph turns to ashes. In accomplishing the malice of his journey, Satan's spirit reaches the low point of its gradual decline, and now the honorable appearance of a martial hero, which throughout the poem has sustained Satan, however incongruously, crumbles away:

> Down fell Spear and Shield, down they as fast
> And the dire hiss renew'd, and the dire form
> Catcht by Contagion, like in punishment,
> As in thir crime.   (X, 542-45)

Since Milton defines true heroic virtue as an inner spirit which Satan lacks, there is no reason to be puzzled by the fine appearance of Satan in Books I-II, or to explain the power and brilliance of his conception with the truism that it is always easier to present a villain in vigorous and vital characterization than a hero. Satan's brilliance is not accidental or unconscious or inartistic, but a precise way of expressing the measure of his decline. He is the archetype of fallen heroes; the Chorus's commentary on Samson would well apply to Satan:

> O mirror of our fickle state,
> Since man on earth unparellel'd!
> The rarer thy example stands,
> By how much from the top of wondrous glory,
> . . .
> To lowest pitch of abject fortune thou art fall'n.

What we see in the Satan of the early books is a recently fallen archangel, who thereupon commits himself anew to sin and progresses further into darkness and self-deception. As we have seen, Christ's martial appearance is not inconsistent with Milton's idea of heroic virtue, because the essence of that virtue is the inner spirit of dependence and charity, and these can be accomplished as well by the warrior's sword as by any other means. For this reason, Christ and Satan are not defined by their martial appearance alone, but rather in the relation of their form and spirit. Since Satan changes, the process is more difficult to follow, but the heroic conventions of battlefield, council, and journey define a sham heroism in Satan as surely as they do a true heroism in Christ. Milton, in his creation of Satan, recognized with Shakespeare the axiom, "When valor preys on reason, it eats the sword it fights with."

THE EPIC ROLES OF ADAM AND EVE

It is characteristic of Milton's artistry that Adam and Eve are not mere allegorical abstractions but, within the ceremonial and non-realistic limits of epic, distinctly human figures whose tragedy seems a familiar domestic crisis. In persuading Adam to work alone, Eve is a typical woman having the last word in a household argument (IX, 205-384). Fallen Adam, petulantly railing against women (X, 888-908), is no less human: as he predicts all the obstacles in the path of a good marriage henceforth, the reader sees a touch of humor in his aggravation, and in some measure doubtless sees himself. He may even see an autobiographical significance, but whatever else he sees, the reader should also notice at this point Adam's complaining tone, his self-deception, and his terrors of conscience, and be aware of the traditional steps of sin and repentance of which this speech is a recognizable part. It is this, however, that most often escapes the notice of the modern reader. The passing of time has transformed most of us from spiritual pilgrims into uninformed tourists, traveling the old road of sin without knowing the landmarks; consequently, we cannot be expected to see where the original pilgrims (Adam and Eve) are at any given point without the help of someone posting signs. It goes without saying that if such a reader is also a provincial tourist – enjoying in a strange land only what most looks like home – who ignores local signs because they are unfamiliar and wanders by instinct alone, he will very likely report back (after losing his way) that local affairs are confused.

An appreciation of Adam and Eve's human qualities threatens

to confuse the larger ethical design of which they are a part. John Crowe Ransom considered Eve's argument that she and Adam work separately as Milton's "passing comment on specialization as a labour saving device",[1] instead of drawing attention to Adam's traditional Christian warning (the same warning is in *Comus*) that "Trial will come unsought ... approve/ First thy obedience" (IX, 366-67). It is gratuitous to suggest that Eve's advice is impeccable, that keeping out of one another's hair is the first rule for sanity and domestic peace. No one could get along with his wife for long if they worked hand in hand as Adam and Eve do, but of course this is Eden, the golden age, when things were different. Dr. Johnson recognized the power and sublimity of Milton's achievement, but felt a lack of humanity in the poem: now we are startled to find that the poem's humanity overwhelms its formal design. A representative modern re-reading, based on ethical sympathies foreign to Milton, is that of John Peter, who argues that Milton's insight into the moods and motives of Adam and Eve arouses such a sympathy for them that their behavior "seldom seems wrong". The fall thus becomes a great love affair, and God, a narrow-minded judge. In this way, Adam and Eve do not so much fall from innocence as rise to a new humanity, and, instead of looking around in Milton's immediate tradition to interpret the lust of Adam and Eve after the fall, Peter finds a more meaningful analogue in a movie scenario called *Lifeboat*, by John Steinbeck, whose kinship with Milton has so far escaped all notice. Adam and Eve in the bower display not simple Elizabethan lust, but something more complex and praiseworthy:

Under the threat of imminent death a man or woman's natural modesty is easily displaced by the craving to snatch some kind of trophy from life while it lasts, and it is common knowledge how this craving can take the form of an imperious sexual hunger. Such a reaction is not so much lustful as possessive. . .[2]

[1] *God Without Thunder*, p. 131. Ransom may have been facetious, but Arnold Stein thought enough of the idea to call attention again to Eve's wrongheaded "motive for efficiency". *Answerable Style*, pp. 94-95.
[2] *Critique*, p. 135. Also pp. 111-12. Taking this position forces Peter to construct a far-fetched hypothesis when confronted by a simile which

Human though they are, Adam and Eve are also figures in a traditional role, and much of their characterization has a meaning conferred by the epic tradition which an intensive psychological analysis of character may only becloud. An allusion to Circe (or Adam's sudden symbolic resemblance to one of Circe's victims after his fall) does not thereby equate Eve with Circe, but it does contribute to her characterization and help guide our interpretation of what she says and does. It helps us decide, for example, that "O glorious trial of exceeding Love" (IX, 961) is not a straightforward affirmation of Eve's love, as Peter argues,[3] but rather the subtle lie of a temptress rehearsing a conventional maneuver of testing the hero's love. A classic poem such as *Paradise Lost*, it would seem, far from being a durable "monument to dead ideas", is actually a fragile thing chipped and reshaped by changing tastes. It is undoubtedly sound and interesting pedagogy to conjure up as many modern analogies as possible – even tenuous and problematic ones – to translate their symbolic and mythical garden into a present-day idiom, but it is something else again to take these analogies so seriously as to remake the moral design of the poem in the shape of these modern configurations. To do so is to create romantic dilemmas in place of Miltonic paradoxes. With such an imbalance set up, it becomes necessary to emphasize once again the abstraction that underlies the humanity of Adam and Eve, and, incidentally, to notice that the moral ideas, seen in their true light, are anything but dead.

The domestic crisis of Adam and Eve is part of a tradition which includes such dangerous temptresses as Calypso, Dido, Acrasia, and Armida, and such fallen heroes as Paris, Cymochles, and Rinaldo. The epic hero traditionally is tested by a

---

makes a logically sound comparison between Eve and Dalila: "They are lonely, apprehensive, bewildered, and the comparison Milton makes between Adam and Samson ... serves only to emphasize the complexity of their case. Eve is not a "Harlot" as Delilah is said to be, nor is the passion between Adam and herself properly comparable with Samson's desire and Delilah's scornful provocativeness." p. 135. Peter ignores the parallel based on the single prohibition given to both Samson and Adam, and the relation between love and obedience.

[3] *Ibid.*, p. 132.

temptress who tries to lure him from his quest. She may be a
goddess on a beautiful isle, like Calypso, who prevents Odysseus
from continuing his journey by keeping him prisoner in bliss;
she may be a possessive queen, like Dido (or Cleopatra), who
wants Aeneas for the same reason; or she may be a dangerous
demon in disguise, like Circe, who turns men into swine. When
the temptress fails, the hero passes the test and proves his heroic
virtue, as do Aeneas, Odysseus and Guyon: when she succeeds,
the hero is unmanned and shamed, as are Paris, Rinaldo, and
Cymochles. Milton alludes to this temptress tradition in *Paradise
Regained*:

> Set women in his eye and in his walk,
> Among daughters of men the fairest found;
> . . .
> Expert in amorous Arts, enchanting tongues
> Persuasive, Virgin majesty with mild
> And sweet allay'd, yet terrible to approach,
> Skill'd to retire, and in retiring draw
> Hearts after them tangl'd in Amourous Nets.
> Such object hath the power to soft'n and tame
> Severest temper, smooth the rugged'st brow.
>
> (II, 153-64)

Satan scoffs at Belial's proposal for tempting Christ because
Christ has a more "exalted mind,/ Made and set wholly on th'
accomplishment/ Of greatest things", but for Adam, this is precisely the way Satan works. After her fatal encounter with Satan,
Eve becomes an epic temptress who turns Adam into a fallen
hero.

The setting for the temptation has an equally long tradition.
Homer's garden of Alcinous is one of the first of a long line of
gardens, whose details became symbolic in the Middle Ages.[4]
Ernst Curtius pointed out the rhetorical formula of description
for gardens – the *locus amoenus* – which forms the principal

[4] The symbolism attached to the medieval literary garden has been studied
by D. W. Robertson, Jr., "The Doctrine of Charity in Mediaeval Literary
Gardens: A Topical Approach through Symbolism and Allegory", *Speculum*,
XXVI (1951), 24-49; Edith Kern, "The Gardens in the *Decameron* Cornice",
PMLA, LXVI (June, 1951), 505-23; Frank Kermode, "The Argument of
Marvell's Garden", *Essays in Criticism*, II (1953), 225-41.

motif of all nature description from the Empire to the sixteenth century, normally a beautiful shaded natural site with six delights of landscape: a spring or brook, a meadow, trees, soft breezes, flowers, and bird songs.[5] This *locus amoenus* describes various forms of earthly paradises in the twelfth-century *Anticlaudianus* of Alan of Lille, and it is also in the Eden of Dante's *Purgatorio*. In the later epics of Tasso and Spenser, the garden itself is a symbolic analogue of fallen Eden – a corrupt garden inhabited by a demon temptress. The details of this tradition also reveal much about the temptation of Milton's Adam.

The Christian poet must have found a readily adaptable prototype for the hero who falls to the temptress in Homer's characterization of Paris. His love for Helen unmans him and causes him to fail Homer's battlefield standard of heroic virtue. He steps out of the Trojan ranks to challenge the best of the Greeks (*Iliad* III, 15-20), but when Menelaus accepts the challenge, Paris' heart is shaken, and he flees in terror. Hector, angry at the shame of a king's son disgraced by a woman, taunts him for mocking his great name:

Evil Paris, beautiful, woman-crazy, cajoling, better had you never been born, or killed unwedded. . . . it would be far better than to have you with us to our shame, for others to sneer at. Surely now the flowing-haired Achaians laugh at us, thinking you are our bravest champion, only because your looks are handsome, but there is no strength in your heart, no courage.   (III, 39-45)

There is a duality about Helen – a goddess in her beauty, but a destroyer in what she causes. The Trojans admire her, but they are bitter about the price they must pay (III, 156-60), and the price is also high for Paris. In Helen and Paris is seen the paradox often found in the Christian tradition: Venus loses her love and respect for Mars because, in possessing him, she transforms him into something less. Oblivious of his honor, Paris thinks only of the perfumed bedchamber, and Aphrodite obliges by rescuing him from Menelaus, but Helen then spurns her lover because he has dishonored himself on the battlefield: "It would

[5]   *European Literature*, pp. 183-202.

be too shameful./ I will not serve his bed, since the Trojan women hereafter/ would laugh at me" (III, 410-12). Having undermined his courage, she now mocks him, "So you came back from fighting. Oh how I wish you had died there/ beaten down by the stronger man who was once my husband" (III, 428-29).

In Book VI, Homer creates the scene which the later tradition often used to depict false heroism – the hero unmanned in the arms of his lady. Hector returns to find Paris in the palace, idly fondling his armor while Helen sits nearby (VI, 313-24). Appealing to Paris' lost honor and sense of duty, Hector urges:

Strange man! It is not fair to keep in your heart this coldness. The people are dying around the city and around the steep wall as they fight hard; and it is for you that this war with its clamour ... has flared up about our city. You yourself would fight with another whom you saw anywhere hanging back from the hateful encounter. Up then, to keep our town from burning at once in the hot fire.   (VI, 326-31)

The Renaissance must have thought also of a parallel scene of Iris, under similar circumstances, pleading with Achilles to return and save the body of Patroclus, "Up then, lie here no longer; let shame come into your heart, lest/ Patroklos become sport for the dogs of Troy to worry" (XVIII, 178-79). Achilles sulks in his tent over his honor, but to the Renaissance he was basking in idleness over a woman, and served, in this instance, as the same kind of model as Paris. Virgil depicts the same situation with his Roman hero: Mercury warns Aeneas to rise up and come away from the queen gone mad with love, "Goddess-born, canst thou sleep on in such danger?/ ... Up ho! linger no more!" (*Aeneid* IV, 560-69).

Helen is a symbol to later ages of the power and destructiveness of beauty (Shakespeare makes a parallel between Helen and Cressida in *Troilus*), but the epic temptress also traces her lineage to Circe and Calypso. It is here that the temptress enters the garden. Homer creates a series of variations upon the motif of the golden isle haven – the isle of Calypso, the wood of Circe, the island paradise of Cyclops, and the palace garden of Alcinous. When we first encounter Odysseus, he is a prisoner of beautiful Calypso. In a scene which Milton later may have used in describing Raphael's descent to advise Adam, Zeus sends Hermes with the decree that Odysseus must be freed to resume his journey. Before he leaves, Odysseus recapitulates with Calypso the seven years of bliss, withdrawing into her cave to take "their joy of one another in the way of love, all night" (*Odyssey* V, p. 75). Calypso's isle is a place of beauty and bliss, and Calypso, a goddess beyond compare, but for Odysseus, it has meant seven years of indolence, and he longs for home (V, p. 71). The wasted existence of the mariner, stranded with Calypso, is suggested by the description of the place. The landscape around Calypso's cave (which readily becomes a bower in the later tradition) includes the trees, singing birds, a vine of grapes, four springs jetting water in four garden plots, and soft lawns dotted with flowers (V, pp. 70-71). But the bliss is ambiguous, for the trees include the cypress – a symbol of death – and the birds are birds of prey.[6]

Not less alluring than Helen or Calypso, and even more dangerous, is Homer's Circe, a demon temptress with magic powers to metamorphose men who accept her cup. Presiding over a kind of magic island haven in the midst of a dark sea, she has the power to charm away the fierceness of wild animals or the troubles of men, "to steal from them all memory of their native land" (X, p. 142). But her alluring appearance conceals a dangerous trap: her cup (a demonic inversion of the communion chalice) becomes symbolic of the power of sexual passion to lure

[6] The details of Calypso's island paradise are found also in other havens, true as well as false, of Odysseus' journey. The Cyclopes' island is a natural haven from the dark sea, with soft, moist meadows and vine stocks that bear forever, black poplars and a pure spring rising from a cave. Of course, Cyclop's cave is a place of danger. The garden of Alcinous is, in effect, the symbolic end of the journey; from here, Odysseus is conveyed safely, in a dream voyage, to his own land. In Alcinous' kingdom, he is rescued and restored, and the grove of Athene to which Nausicaa conveys Odysseus is a true haven whose descriptive details became a part of the rhetorical description of medieval gardens: the garden is fenced about; in it flourish tall trees laden with fruit; a west-wind blows continually, maturing one crop after another; there are two springs in the orchard; and there are well-laid garden plots (*Odyssey* VII, p. 97). Nausicaa herself is no temptress but a beautiful, innocent, and natural part of the bliss, the original ideal of which subsequent temptresses are subtle inversions.

the hero away from his heroic duty and turn him into an animal. Moreover, the dense wood on Circe's island is a fitting classical source for the Christian wood of error, the dark woods of the *Faerie Queene, Jerusalem Delivered,* and *Comus.* Odysseus and his men are lost at sea ("cannot distinguish the dawn lands from the shadowed"), then enter the dense wood of Circe to be tempted and transformed into swine. Though Odysseus is provided with a magic potion to frustrate Circe's design, he and his men nevertheless forget their quest and loiter with her an entire year "sitting to table and delighting in her untold wealth of flesh and mellow wine" (X, p. 148). Circe becomes a familiar symbol in the Renaissance – she clearly influences Spenser's Acrasia and Milton's Comus, and is a familiar figure in the emblem books – of the lower affections which could overcome the Reason and transform men into beasts, a symbol of weakness and intemperance.[7]

If one lesson is clear in Virgil's characterization of Dido and Aeneas (sad though her fate may be), it is Mercury's warning that "women is ever a fickle and changing thing". Virgil telescopes several incidents of Homer into his portrayal of Dido and Aeneas. Like Odysseus coming to Nausicaa for aid, Aeneas comes to Dido a lost wanderer. (He even approaches her court, like Odysseus at the court of Alcinous, hidden in a mist.) Dido's role follows that of Calypso, but Virgil makes her a very human temptress, a kind of Helen. In fact, Aeneas gives Dido part of Helen's trousseau, a symbol of Helen's lawless love (I, 649-52). Virgil's Carthage is a counterpart of Calypso's isle of bliss, a false haven where the hero embraces the temptress instead of his duty, and Dido's nuptial bower is much like Calypso's cave of love. Aeneas' heroic virtue depends upon successfully disentangling himself from Dido. She may be a noble queen, but she is not in the god's plans. For Aeneas, she is simply an unworthy alternative to a higher destiny, and in her arms he is no different from "that Paris with effeminate crew" (*Aeneid* IV, 215), as jealous King Iarbas calls him. Angry that Aeneas "loiters . . .

---

[7]   Merritt Y. Hughes, "Spenser's Acrasia and the Circe of the Renaissance", *Journal of the History of Ideas,* IV (Oct., 1943), 381-99.

among a hostile race, and casts not a glance on his Ausonian children", Zeus sends Mercury to dislodge him from Carthage; finally Aeneas "burns to flee away and leave this pleasant land, aghast at the high warning and divine ordinance". But he must somehow tell the jealous and perceptive queen: Virgil portrays the quandary of the now resolute hero involved with recriminations he cannot handle from the passionate and voluble queen, in the same way that Shakespeare later presents a resolute Antony crumbling under Cleopatra's biting sarcasm and passionate pleading. Aeneas is an epic hero because he leaves her, Antony, a tragic hero because he does not.

These details of the hero's encounter with a temptress in the classical epics were well-suited to a rationalistic psychology and to literary representations of Christian concepts of sin. When Right Reason, the faculty of moral choice, abdicates its sovereignty and loses the perpetual battle with the passions for control of the Will, the individual sins; he discovers, like Odysseus' men whom Circe transformed into swine, that the Image of God has forsaken him. As Michael comments, with a glance at Eve:

> Thir Maker's Image . . . then
> Forsook them, when themselves they vilified
> To serve ungovern'd appetite, and took
> His Image whom they served, a brutish vice
> Inductive mainly to the sin of *Eve*.   (*P.L.* XI, 515-19)

The abdication of Right Reason is often depicted as making a wrong choice or seeking a false good, since the desires are by definition unstable and capricious. A natural Christian symbol for the compelling lure of the senses was a woman, often a temptress who entices the hero away from his proper end and turns him into an effeminate slave. Traditionally, Adam, Eve, and the Serpent symbolize the process. The motion of the senses (Satan) tempts the sensitive soul (Eve), who in turn tempts the rational soul (Adam) to disobey God and choose falsely. Citing Augustine, Saint Thomas universalizes the sin of Adam:

Now in every kind of sin we find the same order as in the first temptation. For according to Augustine (De Trin. xii, 12), it begins with the concupiscence of sin in the sensuality, signified by the serpent; extends to the lower reason, by pleasure, signified by the woman; and reaches the higher reason by consent in the sin, signified by the man. Therefore the order of the first temptation was fitting. *I answer that* Man is composed of a two-fold nature, intellective and sensitive. Hence the devil, in tempting man, made use of a two-fold incentive to sin: one on the part of the intellect, by promising the Divine likeness through the acquisition of knowledge which man naturally desires to have; the other on the part of the sense. This he did by having recourse to those sensible things, which are most akin to man, partly by tempting the man through the woman.[8]

This is perhaps one reason why medieval and Renaissance literature so readily incorporates the pagan figure of lady Fortune, whose fickle characteristics (defined in Boethius' *Consolatio*) are found in Shakespeare's Cleopatra, Milton's Dalila, and the lady Fortune of Skelton's sinful ship, the *Bowge of Court*. Boethius' picturesque characterization of her became conventional: she plays with men, first flattering them with her gifts, then taking them away; one day her face is bright, the next day, covered with a cloud; if you submit to her, you cannot choose your port but must leave your vessel at the mercy of the winds; and she teaches men the lesson that those who choose the way of the world enter her domain and are at the mercy of her capriciously turning wheel; but that those who seek the narrow path of virtue acquire freedom under Divine Providence and have no fear of Fortune.

A common figure in literature, the temptress appears in a number of forms, often exhibits these features, and has similar consequences. In Chaucer's *Nun's Priest's Tale*, Pertelote is a low comic version of the temptress in the garden. Chauntecleer's superior reason falls prey to her beauty and feminine persuasiveness, and he falls prey to the fox. In giving up the sovereignty to Pertelote, he puts himself under the power of Venus and lady Fortune:

> O Venus, that art goddesse of plesaunce,
> Syn that thy servant was this Chauntecleer,
> And in thy servyce dide al his poweer.

The moral of the tale is the lesson of Adam and Eve – the same lesson which the epic presents in a high and august manner:

[8] *Summa Theologica* IIa, IIae Q. 165 Art. 2. p. 1871.

> Wommannes conseil broghte us first to wo,
> And made Adam fro Paradys to go,
> Ther as he was ful myrie and wel at ese.

In *Jerusalem Delivered* Chauntecleer's temptation in the barn-yard is rehearsed on the grand scale of a Christian army and a magic wood: Jerusalem is safe in pagan hands so long as the temptress Armida is successful. Satan advises Hidroart the wizard that the best way to foil the Christian forces is to employ his niece, Armida, "To all deceit she could her beauty frame,/ False, fair, and young, a virgin and a witch" (IV, 23). Armida is to "assay/ All subtle sleights that women use in love" to conquer the knights, in effect, becoming a Christian version of Circe:

> Medea or false Circe changed not
> So far the shapes of men, as her eyes spreading
> Alter'd their hearts, and with her siren's sound.
> In lust their minds, their hearts in love, she drown'd.
>
> (IV, 86)

She afflicts Godfredo's knights with the lover's malady, tormented " 'twixt frost and fire,/ 'Twixt hope and restless fear" (IV, 93), and they soon become unfit to fight.

The subsequent action reveals a process of redemption, as Godfredo and his knights mend their tattered virtue. Godfredo's sovereignty must be restored, and Rinaldo must be rescued from Armida's garden paradise, for only he can overcome the evil spell in the magic wood. Her garden has all the traditional ingredients – "verdant groves, sweet shades, and mossy rocks/ With caves and fountains, flowers, herbs and trees" (XIV, 59). She binds Rinaldo with flowers and takes him to 'a sole and desert isle', very much like that island of Calypso, where "in perpetual sweet, and flow'ring spring,/ She lives at ease, and 'joys her lord at will" (XIV, 71). On the door of Armida's castle is the lesson – a scene depicting the shameful flight from battle of Antony, into the gypsy arms of Cleopatra:

> Antonius eke himself to fight betook,
> The empire lost to which he would aspire;
> Yet fled not he, nor fight for fear forsook,
> But follow'd her, drawn on by fond desire:
> Well might you see, within his troubled look,

> Strive and contend love, courage, shame and ire;
> Oft look'd he back, oft gazed he on the fight,
> But oft'ner on his mistress and her flight.   (XVI, 6)

The rescue of the hero from this predicament in Homer and Virgil becomes, in the Christian epic, symbolic of Grace – the chance for rebirth. Ubaldo will rescue him, but only if Rinaldo will then remember his duty and noble lineage; Ubaldo scorns him as a 'carpet champion for a wanton dame' and calls him to his duty, "Up! Up! our camp and Godfrey for thee send" (XVI, 33). Armida then acts like a possessive Dido trying to hold her hero – at once scornful, pleading, subtle, and grief-stricken – until she finally curses him and rejoins the pagans. Rinaldo's first test in regaining his lost virtue is to enter the dark wood and destroy the spell. He must meet Armida again, resist her temptations, and purge her corrupted garden before he may work in God's service (XVIII, 7-9).

Spenser's Cymochles has all the attributes of a martial hero (*F.Q.* II, vi, 26), but he is a false knight who fights for glory alone, and, of course, he is found relaxing in the luxury of Acrasia's bower:

> . . . for he by kynd
> Was given all to lust and loose living,
> When ever his fiers handes he free mote fynd:
> And now he has pourd out his ydle mynd
> In daintie delices and lavish joyes.   (II, vi, 38)

His squire calls him out of idleness, "Up, up! thou womanish weake knight,/ That here in ladies lap entombed art,/ Unmindful of thy praise and prowest might", but Cymochles, an emblem of intemperance, goes from one garden trap to another – from Acrasia's bower to Phaedria's fertile isle – and learns nothing from the experience. In clear contrast is heroic Guyon, whose quest to purge Acrasia's garden is analogous to Redcrosse's battle with the dragon, Godfredo's siege of Jerusalem, and ultimately, Christ's atonement which purges Eden of Sin and Death. He faces the traditional temptations in the garden of Proserpina, whose beautiful trees, shaded arbor, and running water conceal death and corruption (II, vii, 51), and he is able to reach, with the help of his palmer, Reason, the island Eden, the 'sacred soile where all our perills grow'. Of course, it is now inhabited by Acrasia, who offers her sensuous golden cup to weary travelers. Like Milton's Eden, it is beyond compare with other Hesperian gardens – the hill of Rhodope, Thessalian Tempe, the groves of Ida, Parnasse, and Eden itself (II, xii, 52). But Guyon, observing in the figure of a fallen young knight enslaved by Acrasia what the temptress can do to heroic virtue, remains temperate and destroys her false bower, the ultimate purpose of his quest.

Subtle and deceptive in her garden bliss, the epic temptress was an appropriate challenge in an ethic which considered virtue dependent on self-mastery, and in a psychology which made the faculties analogous to the Christian hero and his lady. The Renaissance lesson to be learned from literary paradises was the lesson Sir Scudamour found in the piller, "Blessed the man that well can use his blis" (*F.Q.* IV, x, 8). Vulnerable to the charms of a woman, the Christian hero could become an exemplum of sin or a model of heroic virtue, depending upon his response to the temptress. Spenser explains these common ideas in Book V:

> Nought under heaven so strongly doth allure
> The sence of man, and all his minde possesse,
> As beauties lovely baite, that doth procure.
> Great warriours oft their rigour to represse,
> And mighty hands forget their manlinesse.
>
> (V, viii, 1)

It would seem from this that the Renaissance, in presupposing her a temptress, had a peculiarly jaundiced view of women. Yet this same Christian tradition also makes the woman a symbol of *caritas,* and recognizes that she may be a glory as well as a degradation. The paradox is no different from Milton's dressing both Christ and Satan in martial garb, or Sidney's distinction between use and abuse in medicine, law, and religion. Defending poetry against the charge that it does great harm, Sidney points out that anything which is capable of great harm is also capable of great good, "With a sword thou mayest kill thy father, and with a sword thou mayest defend thy prince and country." [9]

---

[9]   *Defense of Poesie,* in Allan Gilbert, *Literary Criticism,* p. 441.

Milton elsewhere says the same thing about kingship, "look, how great a good and happiness a just king is, so great a mischief is a tyrant; as he the public father of his country, so this the common enemy".[10] And in the *Second Defense,* he makes an important distinction too often overlooked by modern readers of Renaissance literature:

If I inveigh against tyrants, what is this to kings? between whom and tyrants I make the widest distinction. As much as a good man differs from a bad, so much do I maintain that a king differs from a tyrant. Whence it follows that a tyrant is not only no king, but is ever the most irreconcilable enemy to a king.[11]

Joseph Summers has pointed out that in Milton's moral scheme, every "emotion except the pure love of God can be corrupted, and almost every one except the desire to be totally self-sufficient can be ennobled and made divine". Insisting that *Paradise Lost* refuses to make the usual abstract choices between the conventional dichotomies, Summers suggests that just as the theological and cardinal virtues are parodied and distorted in hell, so also the virtues exhibited in heaven can be misconstrued as vices; for example, the most difficult heroic role of waiting upon the will of God can be construed in worldly eyes as Sloth.[12] We find a convenient example in Spenser's temptress, Phaedria, who illustrates that even the Word of God can be made an instrument of false teaching, subtly paraphrasing Christ's lesson "Consider the lilies of the field" to persuade Guyon to abandon his quest (II, vi, 15-17). In this sense, the woman is no different from the sword, the law, or the crown, in fact, no different from the paradox at the heart of Christianity, as an object as degrading as a hangman's noose was transformed into the most sacred Christian symbol. She may be a devil temptress, symbolic of Venus, or an agent of redemption, symbolic of the Virgin. She may be the 'fickle and changing thing' of the tradition of Dido, Acrasia, and Cleopatra, or she may represent the stable providence of Dante's Beatrice, Spenser's Una, or the virgin queen. In short, the double

[10]   *Works,* V. 18-19.
[11]   *Works,* VIII. 25.
[12]   *The Muse's Method,* pp. 28-29.

image of woman may serve in the same way as Milton's double image of martial heroism – in Christ, an image of heroic virtue in action, in Satan, an image of false heroism. Milton's Eve has been studied as temptress and also as redemptrix, but, in fact, she appears in both roles [13] – a temptress after she has succumbed to Satan, and a redemptive figure after the fall.

If Eve is both temptress and redeemer, what of Adam's role? Adam is no callow youth, but an impressive and majestic figure, "God-like erect, with native Honour clad"; he has the active and contemplative virtues of the Christian hero ("For contemplation and valour form'd") and he manifests the obedience necessary to Christian strength. For this reason, Satan avoids him:

> Whose higher intellectual more I shun,
> And strength, of courage haughty, and of limb
> Heroic built, though of terrestrial mould,
> For not informidable, exempt from wound,
> I not.   (IX, 483-87)

But Adam falls, and Milton's preparation to "change/ Those [epic] Notes to Tragic" in Book IX clearly introduces an event that is tragic rather than heroic. In view of this, it is necessary to consider Adam in the tragic pattern of Samson, and to accept at face value the parallels Milton establishes. To be sure, the term 'tragedy' admits of many diverse views: it means to some a fallen hero, one who betrays the noble nature he possesses; but to others it is essentially a dilemma which traps a noble figure by restricting him to untenable options; and related to this is the hero who suffers a tragic fate because he chooses nobly. It is possible to interpret Adam's tragedy from any one of these points of view, and to consider Adam the archetypal tragic hero for very different reasons. In this respect, our response to Adam's choice between love for Eve and obedience to God is related to premises we hold about tragedy. Some are drawn quite naturally to feel that Adam's tragic choice is a noble act of love,[14] implying that

[13] Frank Kermode notices the paradox of Eve as destroyer and giver of life. *The Living Milton*, p. 120.
[14] Cf. Kenneth Muir, *John Milton* (New York, 1955), p. 158; Waldock, p. 52; Peter, pp. 130-31; Empson says that what Adam sets out to do is "to comfort his wife by his solidarity with her". *Milton's God*, p. 188.

he suffers a tragic fate because of his virtues, which in turn calls
into question the wisdom and justice of Providence. The more
traditional view is that Adam's fall was "no light, trivial, or single
sin, but indeed a *mass* or *heap* of heinous, horrid, and manifold
impieties, even to a violation of the whole Decalogue".[15] This
view is supported by a number of epic conventions which cast
Adam in the role of a hero failing the test.

Milton's Eden is a conventional epic garden – high on a hill,
surrounded by 'thicket overgrown, grotesque and wild', and a
'verdurous wall' (IV, 134-43). As in the garden of Alcinous,
there are trees of 'noblest kind', grazing flocks, green lawns,
blooming 'Ambrosial fruit/ Of vegetable Gold', a fountain, and
birds singing. The animals live together peacefully, the rose has
no thorns, and the atmosphere suggests the beauty and pleasure
of the perfumed East (IV, 159-65). Two features in particular
define the garden: it is a natural spot, untouched by Art, and a
true garden, as opposed to a feigned one. Milton says that Eden
is a spot "more delicious than those Gardens feign'd/ Or of reviv'd
Adonis, or renown'd Alcinous, host of old Laertes' son" (IX,
439-40). The allusion distinguishes between 'Gardens feign'd'
(the false gardens of Armida and Acrasia) and true gardens of
innocence and bliss such as Spenser's garden of Adonis and
Homer's garden of Alcinous. Milton's Eden, like the garden of
Adonis ("There was a pleasaunt arber, not by art,/ But of the
trees own inclination made") is also a natural spot, untouched
by Art:

> Flow'rs worthy of Paradise which not nice Art
> In beds and curious Knots, but Nature boon
> Pour'd forth profuse on Hill and Dale and Plain.
>   (IV, 241-43)

It is a wilderness of sweets where Nature "played at will/ Her

---

[15]   Robert Mosson, *Sion's Prospect* (1653), p. 63. Quoted in C. A. Patrides,
Milton and the Christian Tradition, p. 103. Patrides also cites *De Doctrina*
(*Works* XV, 181-83) where Milton says that Adam's act involved "distrust
in the divine veracity, and a proportionate credulity in the assurances of
Satan; unbelief; ingratitude; disobedience; gluttony; [and] ... excessive
uxoriousness".

Virgin Fancies, pouring forth more sweet,/ Wild above Rule or Art, enormous bliss" (V, 295-97).[16]

Some recoil from such bliss or conclude (for various reasons) that it is too much of a good thing; others, with an unhistorical idea of Puritanism, look for irony because Milton's paradise is such a sensuous delight, a violation of Puritan rigor. Even though it is the setting for Adam's fall, however, there is no evidence that Milton looks upon his rich garden ambiguously or with reservations. He is simply recreating the garden which is the ideal model for all the others; those epic gardens feigned by art and inhabited by a temptress are counterparts in the fallen world of Eve's original paradise. The true primal Eden can be as sensuous and rich as the spurious imitations because delight is not the point at issue.

For Milton, Tasso, and Spenser, all gardens – false as well as true – are delightful and beautiful, and all manifest the conventional details of the *locus amoenus*. But there is an important difference which is defined in the terms 'Nature' and 'Art'.[17] In a true paradise such as the original Eden, Art is as superfluous as Law, for Nature is transcendent, perfect, original, and self-sufficient. In such a case, Art connotes imperfection and artifice, and is often depicted as an inferior imitator:

> Each method Art doth closely watch
> And painfully essay to catch
> Of Nature's working, as an ape
> His doings upon man's doth shape;

---

[16] A variation on this is Spenser's description of Art supplying to the garden of Adonis whatever pre-eminent Nature has left undone (*F.Q.* IV, x, 21).

[17] Edward William Tayler traces the wide range of applications of these two terms in Western thought: very often Nature and Art were complementary, neither one being able to achieve perfection without the other; Art was sometimes elevated over Nature, signifying man's erected wit, only partially impaired by the fall and capable of reconstructing the ruins of what corrupted Nature has lost, in which case Nature signified the unformed, chaotic and corrupted; a third tradition elevated Nature to mean the unspoiled, pristine perfection of the golden age, and Art signified (as it does in the epic garden) false imitation and the operation of corrupted reason. *Nature and Art in Renaissance Literature* (New York, 1964).

> But vainly, vainly, Art may try
> To come near Nature's mastery.[18]

In the epics of Spenser, Tasso, and Milton, the false gardens are counterfeited and made beautiful by Art, the true paradises are perfected by Nature.[19] Thus Tasso describes Armida's false garden with all the conventional details (XVI, 9-12), but Art has subtly counterfeited an imitation so that it *seems* natural, "Nowhere appear'd the art which all this wrought:"

> So with the rude the polished mingled was,
> That natural seem'd all, and every part
> Nature would craft in counterfeiting pass,
> And imitate her imitator art.   (XVI, 10)

Spenser's dangerous Bower of Bliss has the delicacies and delights of true gardens, but it too is a false artifice, "Art, stryving to compayre/ With Nature, did an arber greene dispred" (II, vi, 29). Acrasia's bower is a place "pickt out by choyce of best alyve/ That Nature's worke by art can imitate", and Art makes it abound, like paradise, with everything that is sweet and pleasing (II, xii, 42). Spenser says that Art has done her work so subtly that one would have thought that Nature and Art combined to adorn the garden (XII, xii, 59). Since the demonic garden is a subtle imitation of what God provided naturally in Eden, the parallels are no reflection on the natural model itself. The garden is merely as impressive as are Adam and Eve themselves.

In fact, the same 'natural' state characterizes Adam and Eve enjoying the pleasures of harmonious love in the same full measure as Nature has provided other delights, and without such postlapsarian expedients as law, marriage, or honor. Theirs is a 'native Honour' of primal innocence, not the tainted honor of fallen man:

> Nor those mysterious parts were then conceal'd,
> Then was not guilty shame: dishonest shame
> Of nature's works, honour dishonorable,

---

[18] *The Romance of the Rose*, trans. and ed. F. S. Ellis, Temple Classics, III, xci, p. 48.
[19] C. S. Lewis notes this contrast between Spenser's true garden of Adonis and the Bower of Bliss. *The Allegory of Love* (London, 1936), pp. 327-28.

Sin-bred, how have ye troubl'd all mankind
With shows instead, mere shows of seeming pure,
And banisht from man's life his happiest life,
Simplicity and spotless innocence.   (IV, 312-18)

As Frank Kermode has shown, 'honour dishonorable' grows out
of a primitivistic tradition which held that custom and honor
were unnecessary expedients in the golden age, becoming, after
the fall, shabby substitutes for the true, natural honor which
existed before.[20] The idea is found in the *locus classicus* of gardens of bliss, the chorus "O bella eta de l'ore" in Tasso's *Aminta:*

... because that empty name without a substance, that idol of deceit
and hypocrisy, which by the mad crowd was afterwards called Honour
and made the tyrant of our nature, had not yet mixed its dark con-
ceits with the blessed sweetness of the loving crowd of the human
race.

Love in Eden is an ennobling, temperate, consummated love joined by a concord expressed in our view of them "talking hand in
hand alone . . ./ On to thir blissful Bower" (IV, 689-90), and in
a natural virtue which enables them to hear the music of the
spheres (IV, 680-88). They love in the same way they worship
God, without ceremony, in simple 'adoration pure'. In the bower:

> ... eas'd the putting off
> These troublesome disguises which wee wear,
> Straight side by side were laid, nor turn'd I ween
> *Adam* from his fair Spouse, nor *Eve* the Rites
> Mysterious of connubial Love refus'd.   (IV, 739-43)

If this were not sufficient to show us what kind of love this is,
Milton's hymn of praise – "Hail wedded Love" – contrasts a pure
consummated love with various forms of love abused: celibacy,
the unrequited suitor, harlotry, and perverse fashions of playing
with love, "Court Amours, Mixt Dance, or Wanton Mask . . ./
Or Serenate which the starv'd Lover sings/ To his proud fair,
best quitted with disdain" (IV, 767-70). The power of sex thus
appears here in the same perspective as the sword – a natural
and compelling fertility which is beautiful and good in Eden;

[20]   *The Living Milton*, p. 110.

conversely, a destructive perversion, in which fertility is a curse
rather than a blessing, in the experience of Satan.[21] In view of the
tendency to see this pastoral existence of Adam as static and
dull, it is worth emphasizing that Adam and Eve's existence here
is temporary and provisional, as well as clearly inferior to the
bliss of heaven. God has created Adam and Eve with the possi-
bility that they might some day join heaven and earth, and "open
to themselves at length the way/ Up hither, under long obedience
tri'd" (VII, 157-58). Far from being created to remain eternally
in Eden, Adam must rise or descend depending upon how well
he uses his bliss.

In this situation, Eve becomes symbolic of the alternatives of
sacred and profane. There is no suggestion here of her equality;
for Milton, Eve's subjection to Adam is a natural and necessary
part of their harmonious perfection in Eden. As Eve says, "God
is thy Law, thou mine: to know no more/ Is woman's happiest
knowledge and her praise" (IV, 637-39). Through love, Adam
can rise on the ladder of perfection, as Spenser describes it in the
Hymne in Honor of Love ("all sordid baseness doth expell,/
And the refyned mynd doth newly fashion/ Unto a fairer forme").
Or he can descend by way of profane love. Raphael warns Adam
that Eve's beauty is "fair no doubt, and worthy well/ Thy cher-
ishing, thy honoring, and thy love,/ Not thy subjection" (VIII,
568-70), and cautions him that his reason is the reality to which
the beauty of Eve must yield" (VIII, 575). Eve has all the potentialities of Acrasia or the Virgin:

> What higher in her society thou find'st
> Attractive, human, rational, love still;
> In loving thou dost well, in passion not,
> Wherein true Love consists not; love refines
> The thoughts, and heart enlarges, hath his seat
> In Reason, and is judicious, is the scale
> By which to heav'nly Love thou may'st ascend

[21]   Summers reviews the imagery of narcissism, rape and incest associated
with Satan, and argues convincingly the intrinsic importance for Milton of
human sexuality, as both "natural human fulfilment and the natural human
imitation of divine love and fertility and joy". *The Muse's Method*, pp.
87-111.

> Not sunk in carnal pleasure, for which cause
> Among the Beasts no Mate for thee was found.
>
> (VIII, 586-94)

Her double nature is the beauty which ennobles him but at the same time makes him vulnerable. Her presence gives him added strength ("More wise, more watchful, stronger, if need were/ Of outward strength" (IX, 309-12); but the power and charm of 'Beauty's powerful glance' can also overcome his reason and undermine his inner strength. Her loveliness seems so absolute that what she says seems 'wisest, virtuousest, discreetest, best', and he is ever likely to forsake his judgment and follow hers.

The preservation if this harmonious hierarchy depends entirely on Adam. For Eve, being of the imperfect sex, is more vulnerable to Satan, predisposed toward Satan's arguments, and susceptible to his flattery.[22] She reveals a preoccupation with herself when she sees her beautiful face in the water, and reveals her inner desires in her dream (V, 30-93). Though Adam convinces himself that her dream is of little importance, he has been forewarned that it is dangerous folly to let her stray alone. In this respect, Eve manifests the relative instability of her sex, not so much to confirm Adam's post-lapsarian crooked rib theory (X, 884-85), but rather to emphasize his responsibility for her safety. The seemingly innocent separation that occurs at the conclusion of their domestic argument is a prelude to the absolute separation that occurs when unguarded Eve is overcome by Satan. Adam is responsible for keeping Eve beside him; allowing her to stray, he, in effect, gives himself into the hands of Satan. It is reminiscent of Shakespeare's Antony who throws away all the advantages he holds in his war with Caesar, or Hector who abandons the protection of the walls of Troy. In the domestic debate that precedes the separation, Adam's reason clearly outweighs hers only to be immediately abandoned (IX, 370-72). If there is a tragic flaw in Adam, it is his faltering judgment in the face of her persuasive charm, which turns Eve into Satan's path and transforms her from a companion to a fatal temptress.

[22]   Patrides, pp. 105-06; Helen Gardner, *A Reading of Paradise Lost*, pp. 81-84.

Adam's seemingly innocent decision to let her stray alone leads to a more difficult one, as is often the case in tragedy, but before we admire his great love for Eve in risking paradise for her, it is well to recall that he has already violated it by letting loose her hand, a breach which is not bridged again until Christ's spirit of mercy brings them together 'hand in hand' after the fall. The separation of Adam and Eve violates the partnership of true love and brings Adam to the point where he must weigh obedience and a seeming love in the balance. For love is not love that is contrary to obedience, as Adam must finally realize when his laxness in requiring obedience from Eve is expressed in his own disobedience to God. His inability to command Eve (a form of disciplining himself) is seen later in his inability to obey God. The paradox of Adam's love is not that of a tragic hero resolutely losing his paradise out of true love, but rather the traditional Christian paradox that love is free and yet 'constraineth' (II Cor. 5:14), which defines the inseparable connection between love and obedience. Christ grounded obedience squarely on love, "If a man love, he will keep my words" (John 14:23), the point being as the tradition interpreted it, that the spirit of love which Christ manifested constrains one voluntarily to obedience.[23] Thus Adam only seems to be in the predicament of having to choose between obedience to God and love for Eve; the scale is hardly equal, for his love has already lost much of its substance, and obedience is accordingly endangered. Obedience only becomes an issue after he has forsaken the true principle of love that protects her and holds her to him. He has already loosed the bonds of love, and then becomes entangled in them when she returns from Satan.

After Eve tastes the apple, she becomes an epic temptress, "Defac't, deflow'r'd, and now to Death devote" (IX, 901). A symbol of *cupiditas*, she becomes gluttonous ("Greedily she ingorg'd without restraint"); idolatrous toward the tree ("O Sovran, virtuous, precious of all Trees/ In Paradise, of operation blest/

---

[23] Patrides, pp. 161-64. He quotes Paul Ramsey, "Obedience means no more than love, and love fulfils every legitimate obedience." *Basic Christian Ethics* (1953), p. 34.

To Sapience"); ambitious ("I grow mature/ In knowledge, as the Gods who all things know."); and disobedient, now calling God the 'great Forbidder'. Most noticeable is her change of attitude toward Adam. She now wants the sovereignty in love, first imagining herself 'more equal' and then "perhaps,/ A thing not undesirable, sometime/ Superior: for inferior who is free?" (IX, 823-25). She has lost the sense of true obedience, and with it true love. It is jealous possessivenes which prompts her to share her knowledge with Adam, lest she die and he gain another Eve, and for fear that her knowledge prove to be a woe (IX, 826-33). Accordingly, she approaches him deceptively to mask her lies in persuasive-seeming truth, "in her face excuse/ Came Prologue, and Apology to prompt,/ Which with bland words at will she thus addrest" (IX, 853-55). She speaks false of the 'agony of love till now/ Not felt', and tries to persuade him that she has experienced the same marvelous effects as has the serpent:

> . . . that I
> Have also tasted, and have also found
> Th' effects to correspond, opener mine eyes
> Dim erst, dilated Spirits, ampler Heart,
> And growing up to God head.   (IX, 873-77)

And she claims to have done all this for him, "For thee/ Chiefly I sought, without thee can despise" (IX, 877-78).

Since Adam and Eve manifest the natural virtues in an uncorrupted Eden, the usual arguments of the false temptresses of Christian literature – the *carpe diem* themes that virtue and honor are vain dreams – are not appropriate to Eve. The fact that Eden is a true paradise makes it necessary for Milton to alter important details in the imitation paradises of Armida and Acrasia; for one thing, Eve cannot argue, as the false temptress usually does, *as if* the garden were real because it actually is. The false temptress in a corrupted garden borrows the pre-lapsarian commonplaces that honor and virtue are empty shadows in order to tempt the warrior knight away from his strenuous goal and into sloth and luxury: she speaks, in short, as if her garden paradise were the original perfection. But the alternatives facing Adam and Eve in Eden are different from those facing the post-lapsarian Christian hero in whom honor and virtue are necessary for reconstructing the lost bliss. In the post-lapsarian world, sweet shades and fountains often mean only sloth to a Christian hero who must seek virtue, as Tasso explains, like a royal eagle:

> Not underneath sweet shades and fountains shrill
> Among the nymphs, the fairies, leaves and flow'rs;
> But on the steep, the rough and craggy hill
> Of virtue, stand this bliss, this good of ours;
> By toil and travail, not by sitting still
> In pleasure's lap, we come to honor's bow'rs:
> Why will you thus in sloth's deep valley lie?
> The royal eagles in high mountains fly.   (XVII, 61)

In the arguments of Spenser and Tasso's temptresses, the commonplace truths of the golden age are frequently misapplied to tempt the hero away from the quest. Tasso's naked temptress argues that law and virtue are extraneous:

> Virtue itself is but an idle name,
> Priz'd by the world 'bove reason all and measure;
> And honor, glory, praise, renown, and fame,
> That men's proud hearts bewitch with tickling pleasure,
> An echo is, a shade, a dream, a flower,
> With each wind blasted, spoil'd with every shower.
> > (XIV, 62-63)

> This is the place wherein you may assuage
> Your sorrows past, here is that joy and bliss
> That flourish'd in the antique golden age;
> Here needs no law, here none doth aught amiss;
> Put off those arms, and fear not Mars his rage,
> Your sword, your shield, your helmet needless is;
> Then consecrate them here to endless rest,
> You shall love's champions be and soldiers blest.
> > (XV, 63)

Adam cannot be tempted in this way, for honor and law – existing naturally in Eden – are indeed superfluous names. In his primal innocence, warned by Raphael to be 'lowly wise', Adam is heroic simply by maintaining obedience. His mode of soaring with the eagle is to be obedient in the garden. Eve, accordingly, pursues Satan's line and appeals to ambition ("makes them Gods who taste") in a way that makes this sound heroic. Moreover, she makes the temptation a test of love for Adam, a subtle, persuasive insinuation that his wrong choice proves a higher, nobler love:

> O glorious trial of exceeding Love,
> Illustrious evidence, example high!
> Ingaging me to emulate, but short
> Of thy perfection, how shall I attaine . . .   (IX, 961-64)

There is little basis for interpreting these lines as Eve's honest admiration for Adam's devotion; the context rather points up her irony. Eve rehearses the old forsaken lover device of Dido, Armida, and Cleopatra of testing the hero's love. In conventional fashion, she fraudulently elevates a lower form of love so that Adam will make the wrong choice. Hence she speaks with considerable irony of "equal Lot/ . . . equal Joy, as equal Love", and of "One Heart one Soul in both", for there can only be discord with the overturn of Adam's sovereignty. At this point, Eve is another Dalila – jealous, possessive, and treacherous – enticing God's own champion to disobey the single prohibition. Fallen Adam awakens from the bower as Samson did:

> So rose the Danite strong
> *Herculean Samson* from the Harlot-lap
> Of *Philistean Dalilah*, and wak'd
> Shorn of his strength, They destitute and bare
> Of all thir virtue.   (*P.L.* IX., 1059-63)

Adam's uncorrupted reason is not deceived any more than Guyon is deceived by Acrasia; drawn to the 'fairest of Creation' by what he calls the 'link of Nature' and 'fondly overcome with Female charm' (IX, 999), Adam deliberately forsakes his reason and chooses Eve. Instead of leaving her a tragic Dido, Adam resolves to die with her and suffer the fate of Antony. Raphael, it must be remembered, appears to Adam as Mercury appeared to Aeneas, in the role of 'Divine Interpreter' admonishing the hero to fulfill his destiny ("Like Maia's son he stood,/ And shook his Plumes" (V, 285-86), and Adam's destiny depends no less than does Aeneas's upon his response to love. If Adam's choice is construed a noble sacrifice, we have a tragedy based on the

Satanic view of God as the 'great Forbidder', and Milton's ethical framework is turned inside out. Such a view of Adam's choice would no doubt find Aeneas a heartless cad. The event is tragic, and it presents Adam with no simple choice, but he has created his own conditions – the circumstances in which the choice must be made; he has separated love from obedience by losing a rational grasp of their necessary relation, and now finds himself having to make a most difficult choice. In choosing Eve, the claim of love ("Our State cannot be sever'd, we are one") is a self-deception glossing over the presumption that his disobedience will enable them to ascend rather than descend the scale of being:

> . . . inducement strong
> To us, as likely tasting to attain
> Proportional ascent, which cannot be
> But to be Gods, or Angels Demi-gods.   (IX, 934-37)

In both love and god-like aspiration, Adam comes under the governance of the paradox that enmeshes Satan, whose aspirations for glory, freedom, and further evil are not only unrealized but ironically inverted.

Adam finds the fruits of such a love to be far different when love is based on disobedience – shame, guilt, and mutual accusations. In a domestic version of the medieval debate of the body and soul (IX, 1134-86), Eve pointedly accuses Adam for his weak indulgence, and puts her finger on the crux of the situation, "Being as I am, why didst not thou the Head/ Command me absolutely not to go?" Adam has ignored Raphael's warning, "take heed lest Passion sway/ Thy Judgment to do aught, which else free Will/ Would not admit" (VIII, 635-37), and Christ later makes it clear that Adam's choice has unmanned him, and brought him to the fate of Cymochles, Rinaldo, and Paris:

> Was shee thy God, that her thou didst obey
> Before his voice, or was shee made thy guide,
> Superior, or but equal, that to her
> Thou didst resign thy Manhood, and the Place
> Wherein God set thee above her made of thee,
> And for thee, whose perfection far excell'd

Rebuked

> Hers in all real dignity: Adorn'd
> She was indeed, and lovely to attract
> Thy Love, not thy Subjection, and her Gifts
> Were such as under Government well seem'd,
> Unseemly to bear rule, which was thy part
> And person, hadst thou known thyself aright.
>
> (X, 145-56)

Although Eve has played the temptress, the responsibility is clearly Adam's. He concludes hastily that Eve was to blame (XI, 632-33), but Michael corrects him, "From Man's effeminate slackness it begins,/ . . . who should better hold his place/ By wisdom." Concerned that Adam should blame God for creating an Eve whose great beauty should become a snare, Raphael has warned Adam, "Accuse not Nature, she hath done her part" (VIII, 561).

Other details, such as the parallel between Satan's lament (IV, 23-113) and Adam's (X, 720-844), are well-known and require no further comment here, but perhaps worth noting are several epic conventions which further define Adam's role as fallen hero. The first of these is suggested by Milton's characterization, after the fall, of Sin and Death, who approach the earth like the dogs and birds of prey descending upon a battlefield to despoil the bodies of the cowardly and defeated. Adam suffers the ignominious fate of the defeated. However allegorical Sin and Death may be in other connections, they appear here as battlefield scavengers to prey on the race of Adam because he has failed the battlefield test. After Adam falls, Sin and Death are drawn by instinct to the scent "Of carnage, prey innumerable, and taste/ The savour of Death from all things there that live" (X, 268-69). Then Milton describes their progress towards earth in an extended simile of battlefield predators:

> As when a flock
> Of ravenous Fowl, though many a League remote,
> Against the day of Battle, to a Field,
> Where Armies lie encampt, come flying, lur'd
> With scent of living Carcasses design'd
> For death, the following day, in bloody fight.
>
> (X, 273-78)

Sin and Death descend upon paradise to devour everything including man, their 'last and sweetest prey' (X, 609), and God himself refers to them as 'Dogs of Hell', whose purpose is to "lick up the draff and filth/ Which man's polluting Sin with taint hath shed/ On what was pure", until the yawning grave should swallow them at last.

In the concluding image of the poem, Adam and Eve are wanderers embarking on the journey – uncertain, isolated, and vulnerable. The fate of Eden is analogous to the fall of Troy. Adam as well as Aeneas must leave his 'Native Soil, these happy Walks and Shades'; he stands before Michael, like Aeneas before the ghost of Hector, "Heartstrook with chilling gripe of sorrow", at hearing the news of his impending departure, and in Book XI, sees the world destroyed. He must leave the ruins and rebuild a lost bliss, but unlike Aeneas he has brought about the ruin himself. Adam and Eve must find their destiny in the underworld, "wander down/ Into a lower World, to this obscure and wild" (XI, 282-83). Adam is reassured by Michael that man shall "from a second stock proceed" (XII, 7); Christ will bring back "long wander'd man/ Safe to eternal Paradise of rest" (XII, 313-15). Michael also foresees for Adam other journeys among his descendents who will labor under Adam's inheritance. Abraham, like Aeneas, will be called "by Vision from his Father's house/ His kindred and false Gods, into a Land/ Which he will show him, and from him will raise/ A mighty Nation" (XII, 120-24). He must leave his "God, his Friends, and native Soil", and go into a 'land unknown'. The journey thus becomes the basic situation of post-lapsarian man who inherits from Adam an outcast's lineage – the curse of original sin.

In such a context, Milton makes ironic use of the vision of the future. Anchises inspires Aeneas to fulfill his mission by showing him the subsequent history and glories of Rome. But when Michael shows Adam "what shall come in future days/ To thee and to thy Offspring" (XI, 357), the effect is quite different, for Adam is appalled by his heritage. Instead of the inspiring panorama of Rome, Adam sees the tragic effects of his own betrayal of his lineage: a lazar house, war and slaughter, hypocrisy, license

and lust, betrayal and murder. Man will exhibit the perversity of
Satan and the sword shall be misused:

> For in those days Might only shall be admir'd,
> And Valour and Heroic Virtue call'd;
> To overcome in Battle, and subdue
> Nations, and bring home spoils with infinite
> Man-slaughter, shall be held the highest pitch
> Of human Glory; and for Glory done,
> Of triumph, to be styl'd great Conquerors,
> Patrons of Mankind, Gods, and Sons of Gods,
> Destroyers rightlier call'd and Plagues of men.
>
> (XI, 689-97)

Of course, Adam is disillusioned, "O Visions ill foreseen! better
had I/ Liv'd ignorant of future", until Michael gives him hope
and encouragement with the view of man redeemed through
Christ and the vision of the new Troy – the paradise within.
Adam at the end of the poem has a long, hazardous journey
ahead of him, a test of endurance and patience as well as courage.
It is the plight of man with the burden of sin upon him.

Fortunately for Adam, however, he does not have to face all
this alone. God tempers his wrath with mercy immediately, and
in the process of change from rebellion to despair to contrition
and hope, Eve plays a redemptive role. She is as instrumental in
Adam's redemption and reconciliation as she was in his fall and
alienation. The oracle predicts that Eve's seed will bruise the
serpent's head, and Milton twice refers to "*Mary, second Eve*"
(V, 387; X, 183), an association based on Genesis 3:15 ("And I
will put enmity between thee and the woman, and between thy
seed and her seed . . ."), which Renaissance Christians considered
the first premise and prophecy of the coming of Christ.[24] Only
here do we find a love worth noticing, a subdued compassion in
every sense true and noble, and in marked contrast to the emo-
tional effusions of the earlier temptress. This impression remains

---

[24] Patrides reviews the controversy over Mary as "mediatrix nostra et
interventrix ad Filium". Though Catholics looked upon Mary as the redemptive figure and elevated her to the rank of mediator, Protestants were
careful to equate the seed with Christ, and Milton follows this pattern in
Michael's account to Adam of how the prophecy is to take place (XI,
113-16; XII, 147-51, 222-32, 325-30, 364-79, 543-44), pp. 121-30.

indelibly at the end of the poem. It is Eve who turns Adam away
from despair and helps him reclaim a faith in the mercy of God
that Adam so clearly is unable to find alone.

When Adam is first confronted by Christ, he blames Eve,
"Lest on . . . [his] head both sin and punishment . . . be all De-
volved" (X, 133-35). He complains long and loudly to God (X,
720-844), questioning God's justice ('inexplicable thy Justice
seems"), cursing his own creation ("Wherefore didst thou beget
me?"), welcoming his own death ("Why comes not Death . . . to
end me"), refusing to acknowledge God's mercy ("Will he draw
out,/ For anger's sake, finite to infinite/ In punisht man, to
satisfy his rigour/ Satisfied never"), and plunging finally from
the terrors of conscience into despair:

> O Conscience, into what Abyss of fears
> And horrors hast thou driv'n me, out of which
> I find no way, from deep to deep plung'd!
>
> (X, 842-44)

And he ends with the famous diatribe against Eve and her
feminine posterity, which in its reasoning is much like Satan's
spurious view of beauty in *Paradise Regained* ("for Beauty
stands/ In the admiration only of weak minds/ Led captive;
cease to admire, and all her Plumes/ Fall flat and shrink into
a trivial toy" II, 220-23):

> O why did God
> Creator wise, that peopl'd highest Heav'n
> With Spirits Masculine, create at last
> This novelty on Earth, this fair defect
> Of Nature.   (*P.L.* X, 888-92)

Eve's response to this tirade, as Joseph Summers has observed,[25] is sudden and unexpected. In the midst of anger and
alienation, Eve falls at Adam's feet, "and imbracing them, be-
saught/ His peace" (X, 912-13). There is nothing to account for
it except the most evident cause – "Prevenient Grace descending"
to remove the "stony from thir hearts" (XI, 3-4) – and it works
through her. Eve begs forgiveness, "Forsake me not thus, Adam

[25]   *The Muse's Method*, p. 108.

. . ./ Between us two let there be peace . . ./ both have sinn'd, but thou/ Against God only, I against God and thee" (X, 914-36). Eve's contrite heart then has a transforming effect upon Adam, "Immovable" til then: "soon his heart relented/ Towards her . . . As one disarm'd his anger all he lost./ And thus with peaceful words uprais'd her soon" (X, 940-46). In despair, Eve suggests suicide (X, 1000-06), but Adam notices in Eve's sorrow "something more sublime,/ And excellent than what thy mind contemns" (X, 1013-15), and he leads her away from such a conclusion. Together they reach the contriteness and repentance necessary for the journey (X, 1097-1104), a new concord symbolized in our view of them walking 'hand in hand' out of Eden. Eve's role as redemptive figure is also indicated in an encomium similar to that which the angels accorded Christ:

> Whence Hail to thee
> *Eve*, rightly call'd Mother of all Mankind,
> Mother of all things living, since by thee
> Man is to live, and all things live for Man.
>
> (XI, 158-61)

Thus Eve plays a double role. When Adam abandons her to Satan, a fair 'unsupported Flow'r' (IX, 432), she becomes a devil temptress and snare, but when Christ makes redemption possible, she is instrumental in saving Adam from the fate of Satan. Her role reflects what most justifies the ways of God to man – his infinite mercy – for womanly Eve (like the sword, the pen, or the sceptre) is the subject of a great paradox:

> Ill worthy I such title should belong
> To me transgressor, who for thee ordain'd
> A help, became thy snare; to mee reproach
> Rather belongs, distrust and all dispraise:
> But infinite in pardon was my Judge,
> That I who first brought Death on all, am grac't
> The source of life.   (XI, 163-69)

The epic conventions of *Paradise Lost* are not bric-a-brac which Milton inherited from previous tenants of the epic – antique period pieces consigned to Satan's area in order to set off the newer style of Christ (and incidentally misplaced here and there to spoil the effect) – but rather essential features of his theme. Milton's epic materials enable him to make a subtle and important distinction between true and false heroic virtue and to define the fall of Adam. Milton juxtaposes the genuine article with the clever imitation to test the discerning eye of the reader and to emphasize that the important difference is a question not of style but of quality – a quality determined by the spirit within. In the conduct of the world, Satan can quote Scripture with the best of the angels; Iago can lead Othello down the primrose path at the same time warning him against the very pitfalls he is introducing; Comus and Archimago can give a diametrically opposite meaning to such concepts as freedom, creation, merit or beauty; obedience can be mistaken for servility, and freedom identified with rebellion. Thus Belial espouses patient suffering with Michael, and Satan can make the sacrifice of a dangerous quest along with Christ. All this is brought home to Adam in Michael's extended panorama of the life of man: Adam discovers to his surprise that the beautiful people on the plain are corrupt, that barbaric and cowardly motives may underlie deeds of valor, and that contemplative humility may be merely sloth. Nothing is sacred in and of itself. The sword may protect or destroy, and the woman may lead one to moral perfection or to servile degradation. Milton saw man himself as a paradox – neither animal nor divine but a mutable creature capable of being either. There is no stable, permanent human nature but rather a being capable of every nobility or every degradation.

To exhibit true obedience and charity requires knowledge and understanding, which means that true heroic virtue is rational. Though the modern tendency is to feel that Reason oversimplifies the 'floods of human experience' that Art tries to catch, Reason is a first principle with Milton. It is man's only way of distinguishing between virtue and vice within, of avoiding the self-deception which leads him to confuse his desires with his best interests. Of course, it is also a paradox – as fragile and easily lost as it is precious. The heroic virtue of Christ is plainly an ideal, a perfection of character rarely reached and above the common experience. But Milton does not give us one standard in

Adam and another in Christ on the assumption that Adam's is more realistic to follow. In his own life, Milton most certainly followed Adam with the rest of us rather than his heroic model, and undoubtedly slipped from paradox into contradiction on many occasions, but this is neither here nor there; it rather confirms the fact that Nature often has trouble imitating Art. Fallen Adam, at the end of the poem, enters the dark wood on a long and difficult journey – sustained by the hope that at the end of the quest he might acquire the spiritual virtues sufficient to enable him to take up the sword with Christ and quell the dragon.

BIBLIOGRAPHY

Allen, Don Cameron, "Milton and the Descent to Light", *JEGP*, LX (1961), pp. 614-630.

Aquinas, Thomas, *Summa Theologica*, translated by the Fathers of the English Dominican Province (New York, 1947).

Baumgartner, M., "Milton and Patience", *SP*, XLI (1963).

Beowulf, translated by Charles W. Kennedy (New York, 1940).

Bergonzi, Bernard, "Criticism and the Milton Controversy", in *The Living Milton*, ed. Frank Kermode (New York, 1961).

Bowra, C. M., *Tradition and Design in the Iliad* (Oxford, 1930).

——, *From Virgil to Milton* (London, 1945).

Broadbent, J. B., *Some Graver Subject* (London, 1960).

Bush, Douglas, "The Isolation of the Renaissance Hero", in *Reason and the Imagination* (New York, 1962).

Campbell, Joseph, *The Hero With a Thousand Faces* (New York, 1949).

Chambers, A. B., "Wisdom and Fortitude in *Samson Agonistes*", *PMLA*, LXXVIII (Sept., 1963).

Colie, Rosalie, "Some Paradoxes in the Language of Things", in Joseph Mazzeo, ed., *Reason and the Imagination* (New York, 1962), pp. 109-110.

——, *Paradoxia Epidemica* (Princeton, 1966).

Cook, Albert S. and Chauncey B. Tinker, eds., *Selected Translations from Old English Poetry* (New York, 1902).

Culbert, Taylor, "The Narrative Functions of Beowulf's Swords", *JEGP*, LIX (January, 1960).

Curtius, Ernst Robert, *European Literature and the Late Middle Ages*, translated by Willard Trask (London, 1953).

Dryden, John, *Essays of John Dryden*, W. P. Ker, ed. (Oxford, 1900).

Empson, William, *Some Versions of Pastoral* (New York, n.d.).

——, *Milton's God* (London, 1961).

Ferry, Anne, "The Bird, the Blind Bard, and the Fortunate Fall", in Mazzeo, pp. 183-200.

Fish, Stanley E., *Surprised by Sin* (New York, 1967).

Fixler, Michael, *Milton and the Kingdoms of God* (London, 1964).

Frye, Northrop, *The Return to Eden* (Toronto, 1965).

Gardner, Helen, *A Reading of Paradise Lost* (Oxford, 1965).

Gilbert, Allan H., *Literary Criticism: Plato to Dryden* (New York, 1940).

Haller, William, *The Rise of Puritanism* (New York, 1957).

Harding, Davis P., *The Club of Hercules: Studies in the Classical Background of Paradise Lost* (Urbana, Ill., 1962).

Homer, *The Iliad of Homer*, translated by Richmond Lattimore (Chicago, 1951).

——, *The Odyssey of Homer*, translated by T. E. Shaw (New York, 1956).

Hooker, Richard, *The Works of Richard Hooker*, John Keble, ed. (London, 1888).

Hughes, Merritt Y., "The Christ of *Paradise Regained* and the Renaissance Heroic Tradition", *SP*, XXXC (1938).

Hughes, Merritt Y., "Spenser's Acrasia and the Circe of the Renaissance", *Journal of the History of Ideas*, IV (Oct., 1943).

Kermode, Frank, "Milton's Hero", *RES*, IV, n.s., No. 16 (Oct., 1953), pp. 317-330.

——, "The Argument of Marvell's Garden", *Essays in Criticism*, II (1953).

——, ed., *The Living Milton* (New York, 1961).

Kern, Edith, "The Gardens in the *Decameron* Cornice", *PMLA*, LXVI (June, 1951).

Knight, Douglas, *Pope and the Heroic Tradition* (New Haven, 1951).

Kurth, Burton, *Milton and Christian Heroism* (Berkeley, 1959).

Lactantius, *The Ante Nicene Christian Library*, Alexander Roberts and James Donaldson, eds. (Edinburgh, 1867-1872).

Leavis, F. R., *The Common Pursuit* (London, 1952).

Lewalski, Barbara, "Theme and Structure in *Paradise Regained*", *SP*, LVII (April, 1960).

——, *Milton's Brief Epic* (Providence, 1966).

Lewis, C. S., *The Allegory of Love* (London, 1936).

——, *A Preface to Paradise Lost* (London, 1942).

Lord, Albert, *The Singer of Tales* (Cambridge, Mass., 1960).

Lovejoy, Arthur O., "Milton and the Paradox of the Fortunate Fall", *ELH*, IV (1937), pp. 161-179.

MacCaffrey, Isabel G., *Paradise Lost as "Myth"* (Cambridge, Mass., 1959).

McNamee, Maurice B., *Honor and the Epic Hero* (New York, 1960).

——, *The Descent from Heaven* (New Haven, 1963).

Mazzeo, Joseph, ed., *Reason and the Imagination* (New York, 1962).

Miller, Milton, "*Paradise Lost*: The Double Standard", *UTQ*, XX (1951), pp. 183-199.

Milton, John, *The Works of John Milton*, Columbia Edition (New York, 1931-1940).

——, *John Milton: Complete Poems and Major Prose* (New York, 1957).

Muir, Kenneth, *John Milton* (New York, 1955).

Murray, Patrick, *Milton: The Modern Phase* (New York, 1967).

Patrides, C. A., *Milton and the Christian Tradition* (Oxford, 1966).

Peter, John, *A Critique of Paradise Lost* (New York, 1960).

Post, L. A., *From Homer to Menander* (Berkeley, 1951).

Rajan, B., *Paradise Lost: The Seventeenth Century Reader* (London, 1947).

Ransome, John Crowe, *God Without Thunder* (London, 1931).
Robertson, D. W., Jr., "The Doctrine of Charity in Medieval Literary Gardens: A Topical Approach through Symbolism and Allegory", *Speculum*, XXVI (1951).
——, *A Preface to Chaucer: Studies in Medieval Perspective* (Princeton, 1962).
Ross, Malcolm M., *Poetry and Dogma* (New Brunswick, N. J., 1954).
Samuel, Irene, "The Dialogue in Heaven: A Reconsideration of *Paradise Lost*, III, 1-417", *PMLA*, LXXII (1957).
Saurat, Denise, *Milton: Man and Thinker* (New York, 1925).
Spenser, Edmond, *The Complete Poetical Works of Spenser*, R. E. Neil Dodge, ed. (Boston, 1936).
Smith, Hallett, *Elizabethan Poetry* (Cambridge, Mass., 1952).
Steadman, John M., "Image and Idol: Satan and the Elements of Illusion in *Paradise Lost*", *JEGP*, LIX (Oct., 1960).
——, "The 'Suffering Servant' and Milton's Heroic Norm", *Harvard Theological Review*, LIV (1961), pp. 29-43.
——, *Milton and the Renaissance Hero* (Oxford, 1967).
Stein, Arnold, *Heroic Knowledge* (Minneapolis, 1957).
Summers, Joseph, *The Muse's Method* (London, 1962).
Svendsen, Kester, *Milton and Science* (Cambridge, Mass., 1956).
Swedenberg, H. T., Jr., *The Theory of the Epic in England 1650-1800* (Berkeley, 1944).
Tasso, *Jerusalem Delivered*, translated by Edward Fairfax (London, 1890).
Tayler, Edward William, *Nature and Art in Renaissance Literature* (New York, 1964).
Tillyard, E. M. W., *Milton* (London, 1930).
——, *The Miltonic Setting* (New York, 1951).
——, ed., *Private Correspondence and Academic Exercises*, translated by P. B. Tillyard (Cambridge, 1932).
Tung, Mason, "The Abdiel Episode", *SP*, LXII (July, 1965).
Van Doren, Mark, *The Noble Voice* (New York, 1946).
Virgil, *Virgil's Works*, translated by J. W. Mackail (New York, 1950).
Waldock, A. J. A., *Paradise Lost and Its Critics* (Cambridge, 1947).
Watkins, W. B. C., *An Anatomy of Milton's Verse* (Baton Rouge, 1955).
Werblowsky, R. J. Z., *Lucifer and Prometheus* (London, 1952).
Whitaker, Virgil A., *The Religious Basis of Spenser's Thought* (Stanford, 1950).
Whiting, George Wesley, *Milton and This Pendant World* (Austin, 1959).
Whitman, Cedric, *Homer and the Heroic Tradition* (Cambridge, 1958).
Williams, Ralph C., "The Purpose of Poetry, and Particularly the Epic, as Discussed by Critical Writers of the Sixteenth Century in Italy", *The Romantic Review*, XII (1921).